DOCTOR PAISLEY AND MISTER CLERK

DOCTOR PAISLEY AND MISTER CLERK

Recollections of Ian Paisley's Agriculture Committee Years

I P Moore

Dedication

This book is dedicated to Cathy, Rebecca and Ethan.

Mi gente, toda mi vida.

Acknowledgements and notes from the author

First, my thanks go to Wesley for taking the time to read my draft manuscript, and for identifying and highlighting some important issues and mistakes in it. Thanks also to Aimee-May and Rebecca for their helpful comments on an early draft of the first few chapters.

This book is, essentially, a memoir. As such, it reflects my present recollection of events and dialogue which took place over two decades ago. Any mistakes that remain are entirely down to me.

Please note that I have re-created (to the best of my recollection) dialogue and direct speech when this was not officially recorded. This was the case most of the time where Committee meetings were concerned, and all of the time when it took place outside formal Assembly settings.

When there is an official record of what was said, I have included references to specific Bound Volumes and pages of the Assembly's Official Report or to specific Minutes of Evidence for the Committee for Agriculture and Rural Development as recorded by the Official Report. These are archived and accessible on the Northern Ireland Assembly (NIA) website.

Many of the events I describe can be cross-checked against the formal Minutes of Proceedings for the Committee. Indeed, it was my study of those minutes as research for this book which prompted many of my recollections. The Minutes are also archived on the NIA website.

The minutes do not, of course, record everything that was said, or which occurred, in each Committee meeting, and a number of the events I refer to took place outside the Committee setting.

Some events may therefore have been compressed, conflated or reported out of order, but I have tried to record them as faithfully as possible in accordance with my recollection.

In parts of this book, I voice my opinion of members of the Committee and some officials. I comment on things they did or said and how these affected my feelings towards them.

I think that most people have opinions about those they work alongside, and I am no different, although when I was an active Assembly official, I was expected not to articulate these publicly. Now that I'm retired, I feel that I can.

I am, however, conscious that four of the members that I refer to are no longer with us and therefore unable respond to anything that I have set out in this book.

It is not my intention to cause their loved ones any upset in telling this story (in which those members play an important part), and I am sorry if I do.

Finally, I acknowledge that representing constituents is not an easy 'calling'. Nor is it in any way a secure career, and I think that was particularly the case for the election in June 1998 to the brand-new institution which was to be the Northern Ireland Assembly.

I would therefore like my comments and opinions to be read within the overarching context of my respect for anyone who has the guts to put themselves in front of the electorate, and who is subsequently elected to public office, which I consider to be a very commendable achievement indeed.

I P Moore

1 March 2022

Table of Contents

Part One 1999/2000 - The Beginning

Chapter 1: D-Day Monday 29 November 1999 – Dr Paisley springs a surprise

Dr Ian Paisley MP, MEP, MLA stood, as the DUP's Nominating Officer, and said:

"I choose the Chair of the Agriculture and Rural Development Committee and I nominate myself"[1].

I heard a loud gasp in the Officials' Gallery where I sat with Martin (the Clerk) and Stephen (Executive Support) to the newly formed Committee to which this nomination had just been made. I realized, somewhat embarrassedly, that the audible gasp had come from me (the Assistant Clerk)[2].

We tittered uneasily, along with what seemed like the whole Chamber, when the Initial Presiding Officer (IPO), the Lord

---

[1] My recollection of how he worded his self-nomination is not exactly how it appeared in the Official Report the following day, but that Report is not (contrary to many people's understanding) always a verbatim report. I would subsequently discover there was much 'cleaning up' done of Members', Ministers', and even the Speaker's contributions under the guidance and editorial control of the Assembly's Editor of Debates.

[2] A 'Cast List' of Assembly officials relevant to Statutory Committees may be found in the Appendix

Alderdice, asked Dr Paisley if he would accept his own nomination. We tittered again when he said that he would.

I glanced at Martin and Stephen, who both looked as stunned as I felt. Dr Paisley! As our Chair? Wow! At that moment, I felt totally energized, despite the already long day – it was now after 7.30 pm which was much longer than I, as a career Civil Servant, would normally have been 'at the office'.

We were about to work alongside a giant of a man, a legend, a firebrand preacher whose "Noes", "Nays" and (especially) "Nevers" could (and did) carry thousands onto the streets. A man who evoked such a breadth of conflicting emotions among the people of my wee country. And a man who wanted nothing to do with the Good Friday Agreement or the new Institutions that were to operate in accordance with it, which we could only presume included the Assembly's Committees.

I immediately thought that we were in for an interesting ride, and I wondered whether coming to work at the Assembly had been a mistake.

I had only taken up a secondment to my new post a couple of days earlier (as had Stephen) while Martin had been one of a number of Clerks who had been in place since just before the first meeting of the new Northern Ireland Assembly (1st of July 1998) and who had been making all the preparations for the devolution of powers.

I had spent a few familiarization days up at Parliament Buildings (better known to most as 'Stormont') since my secondment had been agreed some weeks earlier. However, like many of the Assembly's staff, I didn't properly start work there until it looked almost certain that we were needed.

Indeed, that had only become certain on the 27th of November when an Ulster Unionist Council meeting narrowly voted to approve the proposals from Senator George Mitchell's review of the implementation of the Agreement. That vote, and today's meeting of the New Northern Ireland Assembly, were the final pieces of a very carefully choreographed sequence of reports, statements and announcements which would finally lead to devolution of powers. D-Day, as it were.

So, we were all new to each other, and new as a team. Everything felt exciting, almost seismic, and there was a general feeling of optimism and hope – certainly among the Assembly's staff – that devolution represented a real change, and that we might be on our way towards a peaceful and stable future.

Life was full of change for me too, both professionally, and personally.

At home, having moved to our new house in December 1998, our second child (and first son) had been born in February 1999. Unlike his sister (Rebecca), Ethan was already a handful, and I attributed my greying hair to his arrival.

I had joined the Civil Service in 1988, having dropped out of University in 1981 and spending more than six years as a Warehouseman in Marks and Spencer hoping to 'find myself'. I'm not convinced I ever really did.

I had progressed up the ranks in the Department of Agriculture steadily enough but had recently been unsuccessful in securing a promotion I felt I deserved. So, it was in a state of great huffiness that I volunteered for secondment to this new-fangled Assembly.

I reckon it must have been the HR staff at the Assembly who thought it a good idea for me to work for the Committee which would scrutinize the work of my own Department, on the basis, presumably, that I might know something about what was going on. A potential for any conflict of interest never occurred to them, or to me, at that time.

We had spent an interesting day on this particular Monday, finalizing papers for the Committee's first meeting and keeping a 'watchful' ear on the live transmission from the Assembly Chamber, anxiously waiting for the most important business of the day to be conducted.

There had first been long and acrimonious deliberations on the very interesting conundrum about whether or not the offer (a few months earlier) of resignation by the Deputy First Minister designate (Seamus Mallon) was in fact a resignation. Mr Mallon had said, on the 15th of July 1999, "It is now necessary that I resign as deputy First Minister" in response to the failed attempt to appoint ministers that day.

The conundrum was resolved, quite creatively, through a 'notwithstanding' motion which was debated long and hard in the Chamber and, despite vocal opposition from Dr Paisley, his party colleagues and certain other Unionist MLAs, ultimately passed by a 71:28 vote.

During this debate[3], Mr. Mallon referred to "601 days of negotiations since the Good Friday Agreement was agreed". Given the clear results in favour of that Agreement (in the referenda held, North and South, on the 22nd of May 1998) and the time elapsed since the election of members to the New Northern Ireland Assembly (25th of June 1998), I recall that there was a sense, perhaps even among some the Agreement's opponents, that it was now time to "get devolution done" (to paraphrase a more recent political slogan).

Not all of the politicians subscribed to this, however. An attempt by Dr Paisley and others to bring forward a motion in the Chamber to exclude Sinn Fein members from holding ministerial office then failed, the proposers coming up just short of the thirty members who needed to indicate support in order to make the exclusion motion valid.

With these matters now complete, the Assembly finally (around 5.45 pm) began nominations (through the d'Hondt procedure[4]) for the Executive's ten ministerial offices. The team all wanted to be there, in person, for this momentous event, so up to the Gallery we trooped.

---

[3] Reported in the NI Assembly Official Report Bound Volume 3, pages 2-20

[4] A proportional representation system, named after a Belgian mathematician, which takes account of the numbers of Assembly seats won by each party when allocating ministerial and committee offices

The first three nominations went by without much fanfare, with 'Ministers Designate' appointed to the Departments of Enterprise Trade and Investment, Finance and Personnel, and Regional Development (in that order) by the first three parties identified through d'Hondt.

But things really kicked off when, as the fourth party in line, Sinn Fein nominated Martin McGuinness as the Minister (Designate) of Education. There was much consternation in the Chamber and in the public (and press) galleries at this man, who even then was widely acknowledged as having been an IRA commander, being put in charge of the education of Northern Ireland's children. The Initial Presiding Officer had to threaten to clear the galleries if the shouting and name-calling continued.

Things settled, only to erupt again as Sinn Fein, as the eighth party under d'Hondt, nominated Bairbre de Brun as Minister for Health, Social Services and Public Safety. In hindsight, I think it mattered little which portfolios were chosen by Sinn Fein. It was their inclusion in the process at all (as perceived apologists for the IRA and its murderous campaign) that was anathema to many.

Amidst the pandemonium, I was somewhat amused by the fact that the portfolio of Agriculture and Rural Development (my home department) was the last ministerial office to be chosen. It was clearly not seen as a 'sexy' portfolio, and there was little reaction in the Chamber when that office was finally filled by Brid Rodgers from the SDLP.

The whole process took ages, as several nominating officers used the full period of time allowed to them before their decision had to be announced. Once the list of ministers' jobs was completed, the IPO secured leave of the Assembly to adjourn to allow Members (and hungry staff) to get something to eat.

Fed and watered, Members returned to the Chamber about an hour later to carry on with the business of setting up of ten shadow Statutory Committees and for the appointments to the offices of Chair and Deputy Chair to each of these Committees. Back we went into the Gallery, for this was where our real interest, as Committee staff, lay.

There had been some rumours that the Reverend Willie McCrea may be nominated for the Agriculture and Rural Development Committee, and that had filled us with dread, but we had no idea of the order in which Committee offices would be picked. Furthermore, parties couldn't choose to nominate a Chair or Deputy Chair of a Committee if one of its MLAs had been appointed as the Minister in charge of that portfolio, so we knew that this would now influence the nominating officers' decisions.

Given the controversial Ministerial appointment of Martin McGuinness, we weren't surprised that the Chair of the Education Committee was nominated first by the Ulster Unionist Party. The Regional Development Chair was next to go (to the SDLP). Then, it was the DUP's and Dr Paisley's turn, and our turn for consternation. There had been no rumours at all that the 'big man' planned to give himself a job, and we were truly stunned when he did.

The rumoured potential Chairman for our Committee, DUP Member Willie McCrea, later accepted the nomination as Chair of the Environment Committee. Not long after that, George Savage of the Ulster Unionist Party accepted his party's nomination to the position of Deputy Chairman to the Agriculture and Rural Development Committee (the first Deputy role to be appointed).

Our Committee's two main posts were now filled, and our new jobs were about to start in earnest.

Chapter 2: Later that evening and the following days – our first meeting with the Paisleys

The Assembly sitting was suspended at 8.46 pm that Monday night, with the promise that a full list of Ministers, Chairs and Deputy Chairs would be made available to Members within 15 minutes.

There was also a meeting arranged immediately after the Assembly sitting, at which the new holders of Chair and Deputy Chair positions could meet the Clerks to the respective Committees. My recollection is that we may have had a short meeting with Dr Paisley, but that he had breezed out of the building as soon he possibly could, since he had earlier mentioned, in the Chamber, that he had House of Commons business to attend (as an MP) the following day.

When the Assembly's sitting was resumed at 10.30 am on Tuesday 30 November, it was suspended almost immediately ('by leave of the Assembly') to allow the party Whips to agree the membership of the ten Statutory Committees.

This wasn't an easy process, since Standing Orders[5] required that each Committee had to comprise eleven members (including the Chair and Deputy Chair), that every MLA who wasn't a Minister was to be offered a place on a Statutory Committee, and that membership of Committees (both in individual Committees and across all Committees) was to be (as far as possible) in proportion to relative party strengths within the Assembly.

However, the parties demonstrated a surprising willingness to co-operate in this regard and, with much help and diplomacy from the Initial Presiding Officer and his staff, and (I presume) from assorted Assembly Clerks, names for all ten Statutory Committees were announced when the Assembly sitting resumed shortly after 4pm. I now find it odd that there was no approval motion for Committee membership put before the Assembly, but then, I suppose, none was specifically required within Standing Orders.

In addition to the Chair and Deputy Chair, we now knew that 'our' appointments were: Billy Armstrong (UUP); PJ Bradley (SDLP); Boyd Douglas (UUAP); David Ford (Alliance); Denis Haughey (SDLP); Gerry McHugh (SF); Gardiner Kane (DUP); Francie Molloy (SF); and Ian Paisley Junior (DUP).

Other than the interesting fact that Ian Paisley Junior was joining his father on the Committee, the main notable thing for us as Committee staff was that we had six different parties

---

[5] Standing Orders detail procedures which regulate the way the NI Assembly carries out its business.

represented on our Committee, and that two of the members were from Sinn Fein. We were very keen to find out how the dynamics of the Committee would pan out with it having a DUP Chair (and the Party leader, to boot) given that party's insistence that it would not work with Sinn Fein.

Although I am not clear on the precise timing of my first real meeting with the Chairman, I know it was very soon after the Committee membership had been announced, and I recollect that it took place in Dr Paisley's 'Party leader' room in Parliament Buildings.

Strangely, given the shortage of office space in Parliament Buildings, Dr Paisley had, by that point, been allocated three different offices: one as an MLA, one as party leader and now a third as newly-appointed Committee Chair. Occasionally, over the next couple of years, we would meet in the Chairman's room shortly before a Committee meeting, but most of our interactions were in his party leader's office.

I joined Martin (the Clerk) in the corridor outside this room ahead of our meeting, and I remember being impressed (and a little thrilled) at seeing Dr Paisley's entourage breeze along the corridor towards us. The man had serious presence, which was helped by the size of the group, which included his son, some party staff, and two burly RUC minders, or Close Protection Officers (CPOs) to give them their proper titles.

These CPOs, whom Dr Paisley often referred to as "my men", were never far from his side, and they had to sit very long hours outside the Assembly Chamber and the Committee meeting room while their principal conducted his business. Although this appeared to be a long-term assignment for the CPOs (in their teams of two), I never got to know any of their names, really, but they were always very attentive and professional-looking – the sort that you'd certainly want on your side in an argument.

While it was the Assembly's intended practice that MLAs and their minders would check their (possibly) legally-held weapons into the armoury[6] on their arrival at Parliament Buildings, I was, more often than not given their bulging suits, convinced that Dr Paisley's men had more immediate access to theirs. Indeed, I understood that the big man himself also carried a 'personal protection weapon' but I'm sure I remember him telling me, much later, that it wasn't usually loaded. Really?

As well as being excited, I recall feeling slightly uncomfortable that Ian Junior was also attending our meeting with 'the Doc'. After all, Junior was, in theory, just another Committee member who had no more business attending our meeting with the Chairman than any of his co-members. However, Dr Paisley quickly announced that Ian Junior was to be his 'PPS' (Parliamentary Private Secretary) and that we

---

[6] It wasn't widely known, but an armoury existed at this time close to the main entrance to Parliament Buildings. I never discovered if it was just for depositing weapons, or if a cache of weapons was kept there for use in emergency situations – as an action movie fan, I'd love to believe it was the latter

13

as Committee staff could go through Ian Junior in order to contact him and deal with papers.

So far as I was aware, the PPS role was one which related to a Member of Parliament at Westminster and was certainly not a formal 'thing' in relation to the NI Assembly. But who were we to argue with such a pragmatic approach? It had already occurred to us that contacting and meeting with the Chair might be difficult, given his triple role as an MEP, MP and MLA, so this offered a very practical solution to that problem, and we were happy to go along with it. Subsequently, we rarely, if ever, met Dr Paisley without Ian Junior being there too, except perhaps for the short briefings immediately before the Committee met.

The introductions were made, and I rather liked it when Dr Paisley called Martin "Mister Clerk" for the first time. Once the niceties were over, Dr Paisley wanted to look at the list of the Committee's members. My clearest recollection of this meeting is of Ian Junior running through this list of members, making a witty (in his view, presumably) and mainly snide comment about each including the assertion that: "he's a gunman….there's another gunman" as he read the Sinn Fein Members' names.

At the time, I wasn't sure whether or not he was joking, and I thought nothing of it. A few years later, however, I read a report that a DUP MP, speaking in the House of Commons, used Parliamentary Privilege to claim that Francie Molloy had been suspected of being involved in the fatal shooting of an

RUC Reservist in 1979. Mr. Molloy denied the allegations at the time.[7]

So, perhaps Ian junior wasn't joking.

I do remember being slightly surprised and taken aback by Junior's informality in the presence of Assembly staff that he had only just met. This was in sharp contrast to his father's much more formal (and, as I saw it, more professional) approach, which I thought was probably influenced by his long parliamentary experience as an MP. It was Junior's first major political role, which may explain the difference.

I was then even more surprised with what Dr Paisley said immediately after the Committee members' names had all been read through (and commented on). It was something along the lines of: "I think we should have all the members round to the house for everyone to get to know each other and Mummy could make them tea".

As my mouth fell open, I caught Martin's eye and his expression confirmed that I hadn't mis-heard. Ian Junior spluttered something like "No Dad, we can't do that – there's two Shinners on the Committee". Dr Paisley quickly backtracked, but we'd just had our first exposure to the 'minder' role that Ian Junior would play throughout his father's chairmanship of the Committee. I remember

---

[7] Sources: Irish Times article dated 22 November 2007 the day after the allegation was made (accessed through a Google search) and a BBC NI News article dated 15 February 2013 on an upcoming mid-Ulster by-election (accessed via bbc.co.uk)

wondering whether there was more than pragmatism in having Junior involved as a PPS, and whether it had been the party's or the family's idea

Chapter 3: Paul's card is marked

As part of the whole political choreography, a Commencement Order[8] was made at Westminster under the Northern Ireland Act 1998 and powers were formally devolved to Northern Ireland on the 2nd of December 1999, when the "New" was dropped from the name of the Northern Ireland Assembly and 'Ministers Designate' became actual Ministers.

All that formality was mildly interesting to us, but we now had a Committee to run, and Stephen and I were making final preparations for the first meeting, slaving away in our semi-open-plan office on the fourth floor of Parliament Buildings. We had very little idea of what our Committee would want to do or to talk about, but the excitement and anticipation was building among all the Committee teams.

At that point we still felt we had time for tea breaks, and it was shortly after my return from a break on the 1st of December (a Wednesday) that my office phone rang. On hearing the familiar (and much imitated, including by me)

---

[8] In some Primary legislation, certain provisions may only come into force when a Commencement Order (which is subordinate legislation) is made. That was the case for certain provisions in the Northern Ireland Act 1998

voice, there was no doubt as to who was on the other end, and the Chairman announced that he was looking for the Clerk.

At that time there were only five Committee Clerks covering ten Statutory Committees, and Martin was also Clerking the Finance Committee (whose Chair, Francie Molloy, was also a member of ours) so it was unsurprising that Martin hadn't answered his phone, and I realized, with a small shiver, that Martin's phone automatically re-directed to mine as the Assistant Clerk.

As the adrenaline surged, then settled, I reminded Dr Paisley that we'd met, and that I was the Assistant Clerk and I asked how I could help. "We need to get the Minister and the Permanent Secretary up before the Committee next week", he said. "Get that organized, will you?"

My eleven years' experience as a Department official kicked in immediately. In that world, Permanent Secretaries were almost God-like, and appointments needed to be made weeks in advance to ever get to meet one. Getting to see a Minister was even harder, with extensive correspondence case work and the involvement of a Diary Secretary. I relayed this to the Chairman in my best 'Sir Humphrey' manner – polite, reassuring, but ultimately trying to manage his expectations.

That lasted all of twenty seconds, as the Chairman, robustly, made his expectations crystal clear to me. Things were now changed, and the Department and its Minister was now accountable to his Committee, I was told. Things would also need to get done much more quickly than we might have been used to, and I needed to understand that the Committee team (me included) was there to ensure that the Committee's needs were met immediately.

I found myself sitting bolt upright, and my response was effectively: "Sir. Yes Sir! I'll get on to it right away Sir". Hampered somewhat by the rocket now trailing from my backside, I rushed off to find Martin and discuss how to approach the Department.

Things had obviously changed at their end too, and, with a few phone calls to the Department, the Minister agreed to meet with the Chair two days later (the 3rd of December). Although it was the Clerk who attended that meeting along with the Chairman, my own credibility was, I think, established at that point in the Chairman's mind through having made it happen.

I reckon that, whilst it had not been comfortable, it was good to have had that early exchange, in terms of my 'visibility', and I remember vowing to myself that the Chairman would never again need to remind me of the side on which my bread was now buttered. Nor would he have to ask me for anything twice. I would give this thing 100%.

Chapter 4: Dr Paisley chairs his first Committee meeting

While it wasn't of direct interest to Committee staff, there was a fair bit of business done in the Assembly's plenary sitting of Monday 6th of December, and some of it was of interest to the holders of the Committee's offices of Chair and Deputy Chair. That business was going on in the background as we continued to ready ourselves for our first meeting.

Members agreed their designation as 'MLAs' (Members of the Legislative Assembly) and two Standing Committees were established, as was the Assembly Commission which would act as the 'Body Corporate' for the Assembly.

The first three legislative Bills of the new Assembly (on Members' pensions, Members' and office holders' allowances and financial assistance for parties) were also introduced and passed their first Stage, while two 'determinations', covering Members' salaries and members' allowances, were also approved.

It is tempting to be judgemental about the subject matter of much of this early business, and to ridicule the apparent 'self-interest' of Assembly Members. But that would probably be a cheap shot. The truth is that these determinations followed recommendations of the Senior Salaries Review Body (SSRB) which was independent from the Assembly, and, without the approvals, there would have been no authority to pay Members at all.

During the debate on the salaries determination, there was some recognition from Members that adopting a hefty pay increase for all Members as first business, as well as significant extra salaries for a variety of office holders, wouldn't sit easily with the public-at-large. Indeed, the Official Report shows Robert McCartney urging members to rethink "before everyone puts their snout well and truly into the trough"[9].

Up to that point, I hadn't realized that the higher-paid positions included Chairs (an additional £10k) and Deputy Chairs (£5k) of Statutory Committees, as well as Ministers and Junior Ministers, members of the Assembly Commission and the Presiding Officer (Speaker) and his Deputies. All told, that accounted for just over 40 of the Assembly's 108 Members, and so the extra costs were pretty significant.

Those were, however, somewhat gentler times – before whipping up a social media frenzy would become a national sport – and, other than some barbed press coverage and 'letters to the editor' at the time, I think people were content enough to overlook Members' dubious priority-setting so long as they (finally) had the Assembly and the Executive in place, to get on with addressing the country's real and pressing priorities. Mr. McCartney's "trough" comment, however,

---

[9] Official Report Bound Volume 4 page 11

must have stuck with me, and would cause me some trouble when I paraphrased it during a Committee visit sometime later.

While all that was going on in the Assembly Chamber, we were getting ready for the Committee's first business, and I remember the checking and double-checking we did to ensure we had the right addresses for Committee members, in order to post their agendas and assorted papers out in good time for a meeting which the Chairman had called for Thursday the 9th of December.

It seems odd, looking back, that everything was done in hard copy and issued through what we might now call 'snail mail'[10], but technology wasn't so advanced at the end of 1999 – virtually nobody had a laptop, the internet was (for most people) dial-up and we weren't yet in the iPad or smartphone era.

Early on the Thursday, I finished drafting the Chairman's brief and got it through to the Clerk. This was essentially a 'run-through' of the Committee's business with 'suggestions' as to how the Chair might conduct this business (e.g., what needed to be said and what agreement and other outcomes should be secured and recorded). I would nearly go as far as saying it was a 'script' to be followed, but it was always couched in terms that made it clear that it was under the

---

[10] Each member also had a 'pigeon-hole' into which papers could be placed. Some members preferred this route rather than using the post.

Chair's control (e.g., "the Chair might invite…"; "the Chair may wish to seek members' approval to…" and so on.

Quite often, if there was time before a meeting, the Clerk would run through the Chair's brief with the Chairman (who should always, in theory at least, also have approved the meeting's agenda before its issue). I'm not certain that the Clerk and the Chair met immediately prior to the first Committee meeting, but it's likely that they did.

As a final job before the meeting, Stephen and I finished making up the members' nameplates, which looked a bit like Scrabble tile holders but with plastic letters that fitted into holes in the plate. We checked and double checked that we'd got everyone's names correct and decided to be helpful and spell out PJ Bradley's full name (which I'm sure was Peadar John) on his plate.

We also agonized over whether to try to determine where each member would sit, but decided (wisely, I think) to let them sort themselves out, collecting their name plates from a pile as they came into the Committee room. This came quite naturally to them, with the four Nationalist and Republican members perching themselves on the Chairman's right-hand side, where the Alliance party member also sat down, and the four members from the assorted Unionist parties seating themselves on his left, with Ian Junior in the second seat, close to his dad.

While this set-up might have appeared somewhat confrontational along sectarian lines, it was one which was self-determined and which everyone seemed quite happy with. The Chairman sat in the middle seat at the far end of the table from the door, with the Deputy Chair to his right and the Clerk to his left. Stephen and I took up our positions on separate desks to each side of, and slightly behind, the Chairman's end of the table. Finally, we were ready to rumble!

There was a definite frisson of excitement in the air as the Chairman called the meeting to order. No-one, probably including most of his own party, knew how this was going to go, and we were really anxious that there might be a row if the Chairman failed to acknowledge or include the Sinn Fein members, as the rumours had suggested might occur.

I was, therefore, both relieved and surprised when Dr Paisley said, "Mister Clerk, will you take us through the business please?" Martin duly followed the Chairman's brief, always in deference to the Chairman: "with your agreement, Mr. Chairman…". In this way, the agenda items, which were virtually the same for all the Statutory Committees' first meetings, were checked off in a very business-like manner. Nobody argued. Nobody fought. This was quite new to me. Our politicians always argued, always fought.

The Chairman remained in control of the meeting (and was clearly following his copy of the brief, as Martin went through the items) and he found a pragmatic way around the need for the Chair to acknowledge the Sinn Fein members when it was their turn to, for example, declare their respective interests[11].

With his pen, Dr Paisley tapped the table quickly 2 or 3 times, then (with his eyes closed) pointed the pen in the direction of either Gerry McHugh or Francie Molloy. In this way he was clearly inviting them to speak, but he wasn't calling them by name, nor making eye contact with them. That may seem discourteous and unnecessary to us now, but remember that this was in the days when it was Dr Paisley's stated intention to "smash Sinn Fein".

As Committee staff, we were delighted that the anticipated difficulties had been avoided, and Dr Paisley continued to use this technique to allow the Sinn Fein members' contributions to Committee business throughout his time as Chairman.

In what seemed no time at all, interests had been declared, the Committee's terms of Reference agreed (these were quite straightforward since the purpose of Statutory Committees was largely set out in the 1998 Northern Ireland Act and in Standing Orders), and members had agreed to meet in Committee Room 135 on Friday mornings.

This meeting time wasn't to everyone's taste, as many members hoped to deal with their constituency business on a Friday. But that particular 'slot' had been influenced by the

---

[11] These were interests which might be perceived as relevant to the Committee's business and were to be recorded in the Committee's 'Minutes of Proceedings' which were then agreed at the following meeting as the formal record of business conducted.

Chairman's other parliamentary responsibilities, the Clerk's other Clerking responsibilities and the small number of Committee rooms in Parliament Buildings that were available for use by the ten Committees. So, Friday it was.

In relation to the Committee's purpose, a key point of additional agreement at this first meeting was that it was not for the Committee to become involved in normal constituency business. This was a crucial point, and one which I'm sure was pushed by Martin, and by all the Clerks across the Committees. Most of the members had, I think, served as local Councillors, where all business was, by definition, constituency based. But this Committee was intended to operate at a more strategic level, so it was good to have this clearly understood (and put on record by the Chairman) at the outset.

Further business included consideration of four Statutory Rules (SRs) (subordinate legislation) and a crucial agreement to delegate technical scrutiny of these and future SRs to the Examiner of Statutory Rules.[12]

The Chairman also reported on the meeting he had with the Minister (Brid Rodgers) on the previous Friday at which she had agreed that officials should brief the Committee on Friday 17th December on several important issues. While the Committee was perfectly content with this, I thought that having a meeting involving officials rather than the Minister

---

[12] The Examiner is there to assist the Assembly and its Committees and is legally qualified

herself signaled a slight 'power shift' from the way the Chairman had described the new realities to me.

While the Minister would clearly be part of the accountability arrangements, it seemed to me that she wanted to manage the timetable and methodology of this accountability so that it was driven by her (and her Department) rather than by Dr Paisley and his Committee. I didn't expect that this would prove easy, given that the Chairman considered the Minister's party to be his political opponents, but I thought that 'round one' of that struggle had definitely gone to Brid Rodgers.

The Chairman drew the meeting to a close and the Committee agreed to meet again the following day, given that there was a lot of new business to be covered - business that the Chairman had instructed the Committee team to set up. Members seemed fine with Dr Paisley dictating the early agendas, and he was clearly keen to get down to real business.

On our way out of the Committee room, PJ Bradley came over to me and quietly pointed out that he had been, and would always be, known as PJ and politely asked us if we could change his name plate for the next meeting.

I had little experience of working directly with politicians at that time, and I had a slightly jaundiced view of them from what I had seen. I was conscious that I'd need to get to know all my members as quickly as possible, in order to ensure that the team was able to service all of their needs.

I was somewhat anxious about that, but I felt that PJ's discreet manner, and his framing this as a request rather than a demand, had given me an early insight into his character, and it made me think that he was certainly someone that I could work with. I hoped the others would prove equally amenable, but I was not counting my chickens on that score.

Chapter 5: Down to real business

While the first Committee meeting was about technical stuff, the team's preparations for the first week were by no means straightforward.

The Chairman was astute enough to recognize that while many of the Committee's members were farmers, their individual knowledge of the issues facing farmers may be limited (e.g., to a specific sector), and that the Committee would benefit from a wider overview.

While he clearly understood that the Department's brief went beyond agricultural production, the Chairman also saw the benefits of the Committee being perceived to listen to, and to be on the side of, the producer. Producers' debt was an issue that seemed to be high on everyone's agenda at that point.

Dr Paisley's instructions had therefore been for us to arrange a second Committee meeting in the first week and to invite as many representative organisations as possible to brief the Committee on the current issues in each respective sector. He also wanted to have banks' representatives appear in front of the Committee to take questions on their approach to farmers' debt.

The Chairman was also determined to get 'ahead of the game' in having his Committee conduct the first, or at least one of the earliest, Inquiries. He therefore gave us further instructions to draft Terms of Reference for an Inquiry which would deal with producers' debt. Again, his knowledge and experience of the Committee system at Westminster (I understand that he sat on that Agriculture Committee for a spell) seemed to be driving his thinking.

All of this, of course, had to be arranged by our small team, but we did so without any further bidding, and the Committee's meeting on Friday the 10th of December saw presentations from the Ulster Farmers' Union (UFU); the Northern Ireland Agricultural Producers' Association (NIAPA); the Northern Ireland Grain Trade Association (NIGTA); and the Northern Ireland Bankers Association (NIBA) before lunch, and from the Northern Irish Fish Producers Organisation (NIFPO) and the Anglo-North Irish Fish Producers' Organisation (ANIFPO) in the afternoon.

At the bankers' request, their presentation was made in closed session of the Committee, while all the others were made in public session. The decision to agree to this request was effectively the Chair's to make, but he secured members' agreement to this approach at the start of the meeting. This was, I think, both pragmatic and astute leadership.

Despite my years in the Department, I hadn't come across all of these representative bodies, and I thought it typically Northern Irish that there were so many organisations covering such a relatively small population.

I thought it particularly amusing that the two separate fishing organisations could be so similarly named and was reminded of the scene in Monty Python's 'Life of Brian' where characters referred to the proliferation of People's Fronts relating to Judea. Needless to say, I didn't share that comparison with Dr Paisley. I idly wondered which body represented which 'side' of the community, and reckoned (wrongly, as it turned out) that the 'Anglo' part of one name might give the game away.

I remember being impressed at how seriously all of the organisations took their first engagements with the Committee. The Committee room was full of Heads of this, and Directors and Chief executives of that. I guess it was all new to everyone, and no-one wanted to be seen to disrespect the new Institutions. I'm sure that having Dr Paisley as the Committee Chairman also focused a few minds, and he was clearly in his element as they all came to (it seemed) 'pay their respects to the Don'.

As this meeting went on, it became apparent to me that the Committee's format of allowing presentation of evidence, then question and answer sessions, gave the opportunity for members to be able to hear all sides of, and to take a balanced view on, a given subject. For example, far from the banks coming across as 'the enemy', which appeared to be the usual narrative, their representatives were able to explain their position to the Committee, and the banks came across as actually being quite supportive of the industry.

31

I thought this was a significant departure from what we had been used to and signaled that the work of the Committee could well be important and meaningful. That, in turn, gave me a boost in terms of the importance of my role in supporting the Committee's work.

I also remember thinking that the fishing representatives made slightly more of an impact with the Chairman and the Committee than some of the others, perhaps because fewer members had constituents who worked in the industry and because the industry's difficulties (including debt issues similar to farmers) were less well understood and not as widely articulated as those of the farmers.

The fishing representatives also brought a real sense of urgency to the table, with NIFPO's Chief Executive, Dick James, seeking the Committee's active backing for the industry in relation to the EU's December 1999 Fisheries Council meeting which was taking place the following week.

There was a definite feeling among members that the Committee could have an important influence in relation to this subject, and members agreed that the Chair and Deputy Chair should seek to meet with the Minister ahead of the Fisheries Council to emphasise the importance of the outcome for the industry.

Dr Paisley seemed very happy with this acknowledgement of his authority, while the day's discussions also provided helpful context (and justification) for his unilateral decision, before the first Committee meeting, to write to the EU's

Fisheries Commissioner (Franz Fischler) inviting him to meet with the Committee.

Towards the end of the meeting, the Chairman once again moved the Committee into private session, in order that members could deliberate on what they had heard. At this very early stage, no-one thought anything of this secrecy, although later the expectation became that most of Committees' business should be conducted in public session, unless there was a very good reason for it not to be.

At the Chairman's request, the Clerk distributed copies of our draft Terms of Reference for an Inquiry into debt. Members accepted the Chairman's early direction-setting without argument, although following discussions, the Committee agreed that the Inquiry should also cover the Department's handling of recent BSE and Pigs crises, which members thought had contributed to the debt position.

In my (I'm afraid) cynical view as a seconded Department official, 'crisis' was the default cry from farmers, so I remember taking all of this with a mental pinch of salt.

The Committee also agreed to the issue of a formal 'call for evidence' in relation to its Inquiry. In light of the focus of some of that day's presentations on poor prices paid to producers, Members also agreed that the Committee should write to all the big retailers to ask about their procurement policies in relation to NI producers.

When the meeting was finally over, the team collectively drew its breath. There was so much for us now to do, both as action points from the meetings just conducted and as preparation for the following and future meetings.

Among the post-meeting tasks was the issue of press releases. That could cause me some anxiety, since the Committee sometimes agreed to send out a press release without the contents having been specifically agreed. We normally got round this by clearing contents with the Chair (or more likely by going straight to Ian Junior) but I found it interesting that the breadth of parties represented on the Committee were at this stage trusting us (and the Chairman) to fairly represent their views. This was a significant responsibility, and it was crucial to me that we would not betray that trust.

As I reflected on the week, it was clear to me that Dr Paisley had achieved his aim that the Committee should hit the ground running. It was also apparent that he was very actively driving the agenda, but it was an agenda that all the members seemed to support.

With press releases winging their way to the various outlets (in the early days we had to physically put these through the fax machine, one number at a time), the Committee's public profile was also being quickly established, and I think Dr Paisley was very well pleased with the way the week's business had gone.

Chapter 6: The treadmill is rolling, and spoon-feeding begins

When I look back at the minutes for the Committee's third meeting, held on Friday 17th December, they demonstrate, even at that very early stage, the never-ending nature of Committee business. There were updates for the Committee on no less than ten action points arising from the first two meetings, some of which then prompted further action points as they were discussed. There was also significant new business, including consideration of draft subordinate legislation, some of which also needed further post-meeting action.

Although things had only just got underway, and we were keen to please and serve our members, this would very soon come to feel like a 'treadmill' for Committee staff that never seemed to stop (or even slow down) while the Assembly was in session.

The most significant business of this third meeting included a report that the Chairman had met with Department officials ahead of the Fisheries Council meeting, rather than with the Minister as had been agreed at the last meeting.

This may have been of more practical benefit to the Chairman, giving the fact that the officials were presumably much more au fait with the issues than the recently appointed Minister. But I think it was relevant to the whole Committee/Minister/Department dynamic, and once again showed that the Minister was not going to allow herself to be completely at the Committee's beck and call.

Dr Paisley did not, of course, acknowledge the possibility that he had been in any way 'managed' in this regard. He just made the meeting with officials sound terribly important.

The Chairman also reported that he had written to both the Minister and Commissioner Fischler after this meeting, and members were furnished with copies of this correspondence.

That did not cause any problem at the time, but, as with the press release issue, this practice raised a certain amount of anxiety in me, in that the contents of this correspondence had not been specifically agreed by the Committee. So, while the Chairman was purportedly acting on members' behalf, I was concerned that he was doing so without their explicit authority.

Dr Paisley thought nothing of this, but I suspected that it could cause some future difficulties, if even one member disagreed with what was being said. For now, however, there appeared to be unanimity of purpose and views among members.

This struck me as an extremely powerful and positive outworking of the Committee system. Here were representatives of several political parties, which rarely agreed on anything, expressing common views relating to a common purpose. Although the specific issue may have been a relatively small matter, the commonality felt like a major step forward politically, and I was again filled with hope about how politics might mature within these institutions.

Fisheries matters again seemed to 'punch above their weight' in terms of the Committee's attention during this meeting, and the Committee agreed to invite the Minister to attend the first meeting after the Christmas break (scheduled for the 14th of January) to report on the outcome of the EU Fisheries Council meeting.

Members also agreed that staff should arrange the Committee's first 'away day' as a visit to meet with Fish Producers Organisations on their 'turf' in the fishing villages of Portavogie and Kilkeel during the week following the Fisheries Council. Such a visit would again be a 'first' in terms of Committee business (and therefore another 'feather' in the Chairman's cap) and would be a real test of the team's (and specifically my) capabilities in terms of making urgent arrangements.

Other relevant business of the day included discussion about the Committee using the Senate Chamber in Parliament Buildings as a 'set-piece' venue for taking evidence to the up-coming Inquiry into debt. The Committee also agreed to include the issue of retailers' procurement policy as part of the Inquiry. This meant an addition to the Inquiry's terms of reference, which I duly added at Martin's request.

In other business, two members also proposed motions for the Committee to consider. This was very much the way Council business was conducted, and I think that members expected the Committee would conduct its business similarly. That didn't turn out to be the case, but these were early days, and Dr Paisley was content to allow members some slack.

Some members also sought to 'second' the motions proposed. Seconding was a requirement for Council business, but there was no such requirement under Standing Orders relating to Committee business, and the Clerk correctly (and with the Chairman's backing) pointed this out to members.

The first motion was about having a separate cattle tag for Northern Ireland (raised by PJ Bradley), while the second was in support of a case being made for low incidence BSE status for Northern Ireland, raised by Billy Armstrong.

Mr. Bradley's motion referred to markets being open to producers in Ireland but not to the UK, but he was anxious to explain that it was not politically motivated. Again, I was surprised that the Chairman and the other Unionist members appeared to accept Mr. Bradley's stated motives at face value. Of course, as politicians, they were probably more aware of PJ than I, and had their own views on his trustworthiness.

As it happened, advance notice of PJ's motion had allowed our team to contact the Department about it and to brief the Chairman in advance. He was thus able to advise the Committee that the outcome sought by the motion was not achievable unless an amendment was made to an EU

Regulation on foot of a decision by the EU's Agriculture Council. The Committee was, however, able to accept the principles behind the motion and therefore agreed to bring their views to the Minister's attention. PJ seemed happy enough with that outcome, while Dr Paisley was more than content to appear as informed as he did.

Mr. Armstrong's motion was in support of a case that was already being made by the industry (and the objectives of which appeared to be achievable under current EU rules). Billy's motion was unanimously agreed among the Committee, which further agreed to issue a press release about the agreed motion and to formally advise the Minister of the Committee's views.

Once again, the commonality of purpose and opinion among members was surprising to me, and most encouraging.

This meeting also brought the first opportunity for the Committee to receive presentations from Department officials, and to ask them questions. The matters covered were the 'Beef National Envelope' and 'EU Structural Funds' which were the subject of separate presentations by senior DARD staff (at Grade 5 level, often known as 'Assistant Secretaries').

The Department had sent papers to the Committee on each subject in advance, and these had been included among the papers issued to members before the meeting. I made it my business to read and become fully familiar with the Department's papers, in order that I could follow discussions about the papers and report on them in the Committee's minutes of proceedings. It was my responsibility as Assistant Clerk to draft these minutes after every meeting for the Clerk's (and ultimately the Committee's) agreement.

The papers prompted some further questions in my mind, and there were a number of issues that I thought the Committee might find it useful to clarify with the officials.

Having cleared them with the Clerk (who didn't have the luxury of time to be able to consider the papers in full) and, with the Chairman's agreement, my thoughts were committed to paper and provided to each of the members at the start of the meeting. It is possible that this approach was suggested by the Clerk, or even by the Chairman, rather than having been my own idea. I simply don't recall.

However, when members started questioning the officials, it quickly became clear to me that some of them had not read the department's papers at all and that they were relying entirely on my additional briefing. I wondered then, and I've often wondered since, whether providing members with this additional briefing was actually the right thing to do.

The precedent was set, however, and the practice quickly became established. Members expected to be provided with similar briefing around every subject being discussed: "where are our questions on this?" or "where's our summary of what this all means?"

My briefing was always quite deliberately couched in terms that gave members their place (e.g., "members may wish to explore x, y and z further" or "members may wish to query the consistency of points a and b in the department's paper"). I also had to be careful to base my briefing entirely on the contents of the Department's papers, and not on anything I might have known, or suspected, as a result of my having been an official in that Department. Nor could I be seen to have a personal agenda in relation to any of the subjects before the Committee.

I was, I felt, walking a very fine line.

As an Assistant Clerk (and as a constituent) I had quite high expectations that members of the Committee would be diligent in performing their scrutiny role, particularly if being an MLA was their main or only political role.

I will always harbour concerns that such 'spoon-feeding' reduced the need for members to have read (and attempted to understand) all of their papers prior to a meeting and therefore allowed the potential for some shirking of responsibilities.

However, I must stress that there were some members whom I considered to be 'all over' their papers and well able to 'feed' themselves.

Chief among these was probably Alliance's David Ford, whose lines of questioning nearly always came across as thoughtful, balanced and well-informed. I got the sense that PJ Bradley and Ian Paisley Junior were also well clued in while the Chairman had the ability to grasp the salient points in his pre-brief if he hadn't had time to read the whole package (which would happen quite often, given his other commitments).

We were, of course, making up the whole 'committee support' role as we went along, and I am quite sure that our team was not alone in providing our members with such a high level of support.

Furthermore, as a seconded civil servant, I had the benefit of training and experience in the analysis and summary of policy papers, which some members almost certainly did not have. Why should my experience not be a legitimate resource for members who were less experienced in those areas, of whom a lot was being asked?

Whatever the merits and drawbacks of the 'extra briefing' approach, the meeting with officials on the 17th of December was considered a productive one. The final act in the meeting was for the Chairman, who was in very good form, to wish the compliments of the season to all the members.

I imagined that Ian Paisley Junior was relieved to look round to see that neither of the Sinn Fein members was present to accept those compliments, since that might conceivably have been noticed and made it into the papers. All in all, however, this seemed a positive way to end what had been a tumultuous decade.

Chapter 7: A new Millennium, and (finally) a first Ministerial appearance

The Assembly's Christmas recess (staff would soon come to yearn desperately for each and every recess) allowed us all some time with our families. We returned relieved (but also, if I'm honest, ever-so-slightly disappointed) that the world hadn't been brought crashing to a standstill by the promised millennium bug, and ready for whatever the new year would bring.

The Committee's next meeting took place on the 14th of January and the Minister's first appearance before Dr Paisley and his Committee was big enough news for both the BBC and UTV to send along a camera crew. There was at that time no facility for live camera feeds, and it was not really practical for the large TV cameras to be operated in what was a relatively small Committee room.

The Chairman, however, took the decision to allow the camera crews to cover the start of the Minister's session, and then to pack up and leave. He alerted members to this in closed session at the start of the meeting. There was no way he could have been talked out of it, but he carefully sought their agreement, thus keeping them 'on-side'.

At the Chair's invitation, the Clerk also distributed a summary note of the issues that had been discussed in a meeting between the Minister and the Chairman and Deputy Chairman, which had been held (at Dr Paisley's request) on the Monday after the last Committee meeting before Christmas.

While the Clerk had attended that meeting, and members were given his summary of it, I think we were all beginning to feel a little uncomfortable with the authority for, and appropriateness of, such meetings. We felt that Committee business should be properly conducted in the Committee setting.

It was, I suppose, hard for high profile politicians to move away from the hitherto established practice of demanding (and usually getting) to meet a Minister or officials one-to-one. Committee Chairs and Ministers were learning 'on the job' too, as there was little precedent to go on.

As the Chairman gave a rundown (in private session) of the things that were going to be discussed with the Minister, there was a definite sense building of a 'Paisley versus Rodgers' showdown. There seemed little love lost between the two in their previous political lives, with their polar opposite political viewpoints, and there was, I think, a general view that the Minister was inexperienced in agricultural matters, and that she was going up against a Chairman who had significant experience in those areas.

I was interested in how confrontational this meeting would be, particularly given that two Committee members were members of the Minister's political party, the SDLP. And with the cameras there, and general press interest, I expected some 'grandstanding' at the very least.

Again, I was somewhat surprised. Although the Chairman opened with a statement about the Committee's role and the many issues of crisis among farmers and fishermen on which the Committee had already been lobbied, he was also very respectful and businesslike in his approach.

The Minister was able to make a statement covering three important issues, including the outcome of the December Fisheries Council, which had been difficult, but arguably not quite as bad as the fishermen had feared.

The Chairman then facilitated questions from the members in a very fair and even-handed way, and the Minister, I thought, came across reasonably well briefed on the issues. It helped, of course, that any blame for the current crises couldn't be laid at her door, having only recently taken up office. How often have we seen that defence used by an incoming Government?

All in all, the anticipated 'showdown' could only be described as a draw. After the Minister had left, and the Committee withdrew again into private session, I found it quite amusing that the levels of criticism against the Department started to rise, and a press release was agreed which would express concern that members had no reason to feel optimistic about the agriculture industry. They are all very brave now, I thought, but I wondered why they hadn't said all this to her face.

And with the Minister having, on the issue of pig farming, included reference to a scheme in the Republic of Ireland to support pig farmers, I found it almost ironic that the Chairman appeared to be advocating that his political enemies' 'Free State' approach should be adopted in Northern Ireland.

As the last business of the meeting, the Committee agreed to postpone its planned excursion to the fishing villages the following Friday, given that another important meeting was to be held in Brussels on the 20th and 21st of January.

With an inward sigh, I realized that meant Stephen and I undoing and re-making arrangements which were well underway, but I accepted that this was now 'our lot' in life and we got in touch with the Fish Producers' Organisations as soon as the meeting broke up.

Chapter 8: The Committee flexes its muscles, and a new and familiar member comes on board

I think that maybe some members, including Dr Paisley, had time to reflect on a missed opportunity for point-scoring during the Minister's first appearance. Whatever the reason, the next couple of Committee meetings appeared to take on a certain amount of 'authority stamping' on the Committee's part.

Members considered the Minister's earlier comments on the potato industry and concluded that the Committee's forthcoming meeting with retailers should include reference to that industry.

The Committee also agreed to 'mark the department's card' in relation to the need for it to be involved in the Department's consultation processes where subordinate legislation was proposed. This hardening of approach was clearly led by Dr Paisley, but it was agreed without dissent.

The Committee then agreed (I thought strangely) that Ian Paisley Junior should meet with the Department's Permanent Secretary, Peter Small, in relation to recent appointments to the Agricultural Wages Board. I was uncertain how it could ever be appropriate for the Committee to 'interfere' in this process, (or how Ian Junior could be considered as representing the Committee) and I decided to pass on my unease about this to the Clerk. I wasn't sure what he did with this, but the Junior substitution never happened again.

On the 21st of January (i.e., for the second week in a row) the Minister agreed the Committee's invitation to appear before it, this time giving a presentation on 'Agenda 2000 CAP Reforms'.

There was much more robust discussion during these exchanges, with the Chairman reporting a list of the Committee's concerns to the Minister. Those concerns were based on my briefing on the Department's advance memorandum that members had considered in private session before the Minister arrived.

I was by now resigned to the fact that it was expected that Committee staff would provide such briefing, but I'll admit to squirming in my seat somewhat as a number of my (impartial) observations were couched as criticisms of the Department by the Chairman and by some other members.

Having said that, the Committee did take ownership of the issues and, after the Minister had left, agreed its position on several aspects of the CAP reforms and also agreed to forward these to the Minister. With those agreements recorded, the views and criticisms could no longer be traced back to me. I was, ultimately, pleased that my efforts had helped facilitate the Committee's work, as the provision of advice to the

Minister was one of the main statutory purposes of the Committee.

The Committee also took a pragmatic decision in relation to forthcoming protests by NIAPA (to be held outside a number of meat plants) agreeing that Committee members could attend such protests, but only as MLAs, i.e., not in any way representing the Committee. I am sure that approach was suggested by the Clerk, but Dr Paisley was happy to endorse it.

The meeting held on the 28th of January was notable as the first meeting missed by Dr Paisley, and George Savage took the chair that day. The Committee's 'holding to account' role continued in that meeting with four senior DARD officials giving a presentation on the Department's spending plans and being suitably grilled for their trouble.

By now I had started to notice, and be amused by, a tendency for Sinn Fein's Gerry McHugh to use the same phrase during every Committee meeting, regardless of the subject matter. Whatever the sector being discussed, it seemed that Gerry would suggest that it should be "benchmarked against the South".

Gerry never went on to suggest how benchmarking might be done, or what the local benefits might be, so I wasn't convinced that he fully understood the concept he was advocating. It was almost as if he thought that the phrase was consistent with his Republican/Nationalist credentials, and that it might annoy Unionist members on the Committee, and he trotted it out over several of the early meetings. However, these contributions appeared to fall on deaf ears, provoking neither support nor opposition, and after a few meetings benchmarking was heard about much less frequently.

In terms of preparations for meetings, I was starting to suffer from a serious overload of information. Standing Orders were clear that no document received by the Clerk could be altered or withdrawn without the knowledge and approval of the Committee, so it was not possible for us to 'bury' anything, even if we'd wanted to.

I now felt I had to read all of the information sent to the Committee, summarize it and also provide questions related to it when the information providers came up before the Committee. But when DARD sent us a copy for each member of the massive EU-related 'Accompanying Measure Plan' (which the Committee had complained to the Minister at the previous meeting that they had not seen) I realized that there was a limit to what I could actually do, and how much the Committee really needed to see.

In this instance the Clerk and I agreed that members should be furnished with their copies and asked (by the Chairman) to bring any specific matters to the Committee's attention. It was such a huge, and complex, document that we had a pretty good idea that nobody would, and nobody did.

We went on to use that tactic quite frequently, particularly when members asked for more information on a subject without giving any thought to what they might actually do with it, and many potentially loose ends were tied up in this way.

George Savage advised the Committee that he had discussed the Clerk's draft forward work programme with the Chairman, and he commended it to the Committee, who agreed its contents.

A plan was now coming together, with the fisheries visit now scheduled for the following Friday (4th of February) and an evidence session planned with the major retailers on 11th February, with further oral evidence to be taken for the Committee's debt Inquiry on the three subsequent Fridays.

There was so much practical working together going on in the Committee among previously opposing parties and members – encouraged and led in no small part by Dr Paisley - that I was almost becoming giddy!

Outside the Committee, however, the mood music wasn't so positive, with no sign of the hoped-for decommissioning of the IRA's arsenal of weapons.

Recriminations about, and ill-will towards, the Institutions of the Agreement were becoming a daily feature of the news, with Dr Paisley front and centre in terms of opposition (to pretty much everything) and in apportioning blame for it all to the larger Unionist party.

It did seem a bit like he was attempting to 'ride two horses' within the Assembly system, and I wondered how that might end up for him.

I had my own things to worry about. The 28th of January Committee meeting was the first one attended by John Dallat from the SDLP, whom the party had appointed in place of Denis Haughey, who had resigned from the Committee when he was appointed as a junior Minister.

I hadn't yet managed to form an opinion about Denis, but it is fair to say that I was not overly delighted to see John taking Denis's place, given that we had 'locked horns' relatively recently when I was working in the Department's Rural Development Programme.

One of the three major regeneration projects in my area was a fishing lodge in Kilrea, which had a £780k budget and aimed to promote angling tourism in the area. John, then a local Coleraine Borough Councillor, had been the Chairman of the Kilrea Enterprise Group (KEG), which was in receipt of funding for this project through the original EU LEADER programme. I was given responsibility for monitoring the project and its associated expenditure.

Without going into too much detail, the Enterprise Group did not really have the skills to manage such a large project, or indeed the two staff hired to run the facility. In hindsight, this was as much the fault of the Department, whose expectations of a community group were much too high, and the project was fraught with difficulty, especially when it started making significant losses.

I'm sure that the project management troubles made John's chairmanship of the cross-community Enterprise group very difficult. I know I was affected by the stress of it all and, although my relationship with many of the other members of KEG was grand, I wouldn't have counted John as one of my biggest fans, and the feeling was mutual.

He was, however, now a member of the Committee I worked for, and his needs had to be served as much as the others', so I was determined to set aside my personal feelings towards him as I re-introduced myself at the end of the meeting. We made light of our coming across each other again, but I got the sense that I might have my work cut out to demonstrate that I was now fully on his side.

As soon as the meeting finished on the 28th, Stephen got down to finalizing the arrangements for the Committee's fisheries visit the following Friday.

We thought it would be interesting to get away from the confines of Parliament Buildings. It was to prove very interesting indeed.

Chapter 9: Fish (and eggs) on Friday – Paisleys under fire

Having confirmed that there was money in the Assembly's budget for Committees to spend on trips outside Parliament Buildings, we went about spending the first of that money as best we could for the Committee's visit to the fishing villages.

Stephen had set up the itinerary in consultation with the Fish Producers Organisations and when I arrived at work on Friday the 4th of February, there was a shiny new 15-seater Mercedes minibus and driver sitting at the east door of Parliament Buildings, ready for our road trip. Very fancy, and ours for the day!

The minibus arrangement gave the DUP committee members some difficulty, however, since they would be confined in the bus in very close proximity to the Sinn Fein members, with whom the party still officially refused to work. Security considerations provided one fairly easy solution, though, since Dr Paisley's Close Protection Officers wouldn't even contemplate his traveling in the minibus. They decided he was to travel separately in his (presumably armoured) police-driven car and the Chairman in turn decided that Ian Junior would travel with him.

In what I took to be indication of the esteem in which Gardiner Kane was held within the party, he was abandoned to travel in the minibus on his own, and it was quite funny to see him wait until the 'Shinners' were seated before placing himself as far away from them on the bus as he possibly could.

The Clerk travelled with the Chair, so he could brief him on the proposed itinerary, and Stephen and I got onto the minibus with the rest of the members - all, that is, except John Dallat and Boyd Douglas, who'd given their apologies the previous week. My recollection is that it was a fine, sunny, winter's day as we set off 'for the seaside', and I determined that I would try not to lose any of the members on their first trip out.

In early 2000, security considerations were still uppermost in people's minds, and we had been careful, in issuing a press release about the visit, not to include all of the detail around timings. That said, those involved in the meetings were all well aware of the arrangements. So, people knew we were coming.

The Clerk had also made it his business to speak to local police commanders in charge of the three villages on the itinerary: Portavogie, Ardglass and Kilkeel, which were to be visited in that order.

Before we set out, the Clerk told me that the police had shown some interest in the Portavogie leg, which may well have been prompted by the Minister, Brid Rodgers, having been pelted with eggs by 'protesters' during her visit there in December. The police on the other side of Strangford Lough were, on the other hand, very relaxed about the Ardglass and Kilkeel legs.

All this raised my anxiety levels slightly as we got underway, and I was told to stay in contact with Martin in Dr Paisley's car via my personal mobile phone, which was very basic at the time, offering only calls and texts. All in all, though, the mood in the bus was jovial - a bit like a school trip - and Stephen and I did the rounds with all the members, getting to know them a little better outside the Committee room, and briefing them on who they were due to meet.

It wasn't very long before we arrived at the harbour in Portavogie, and we all got out of the bus to join the Paisleys and the Clerk. I think that the Clerk had been speaking to the BBC's local Agriculture correspondent (Martin Cassidy) ahead of the visit, and Martin C was already there with a small camera crew.

I heard some noise, with some voices calling out, but I couldn't figure where it was from or what was being shouted, and we headed towards the NIFPO HQ, to hold a meeting with Dick James, the NIFPO Chief Executive, along with other NIFPO officials and fishermen.

Our initial saunter towards the building was hurried up significantly by the sound and sight of eggs hitting the concrete, accompanied by loud jeers. None came anywhere near me, but Ian junior (of all people, I thought, given that this was a staunchly loyalist town) got some splashes on his coat, or it may have been on his trousers. I wasn't unduly worried, since there didn't appear to be any threat in close proximity, and there were uniformed police officers around.

Having held a short meeting, the group was then escorted around the harbour to see some of the trawlers and the harbour facilities. It became pretty obvious that the BBC team was doing its best to capture Dr Paisley and the Sinn Fein Members together in the same shot, but it was equally obvious that the two Paisleys were doing their best to avoid that shot ever being available.

As we walked past some of the boats, the salty sea air was filled with a loud clapping or slapping noise. At first, I couldn't identify its source, but my eyes were soon drawn to the deck of one of the trawlers. I nearly choked when I realized that I was staring at (not to put too fine a point on it) a big red arse, as a well-proportioned fisherman was seriously 'mooning' the committee while gleefully slapping his backside with both hands. There was a large cry of "Yeeeowww" from nearby as others, who now seemed to be forming into a group, saw what was going on.

Everyone's reaction was to laugh, somewhat uncomfortably, and I think that this very personal protest was over before the BBC crew managed to get it on film, but there clearly wasn't a great deal of respect or welcome being shown in this village for the Committee, with its Sinn Fein members. Nor did Dr Paisley's reputation, as a leader of Protestants, seem to hold much water with these particular protesters.

Our group moved on quickly to the fish market on the quay and, while inside, members were genuinely interested in the selection of fish on offer, the prices that were being secured by the fishermen, and the restrictions that were now being placed on the local fleet. The minibus, and the Paisleys' car, had been moved to a car park close by the fish hall. Even from within the confines of the market I could hear that a hostile atmosphere was building on the quayside, and it was no surprise when the Clerk told me that the police had decided it was time for the Committee to go. He said he would round up the Paisleys, and he asked that Stephen and I start to herd the members towards the bus.

I approached Sinn Fein's Francie Molloy and Gerry McHugh and said that the police had suggested it was time to go. Silly me! Their reaction was fairly predictable: "We aren't going to let the RUC tell us what to do" they practically chorused. The sounds of protest were growing all the time. "Please", I said. "Never mind the RUC, I'm getting quite worried, and I'd really like us to go now". Reluctantly, they agreed, and we left the fish hall for the sanctuary of the minibus.

We could see (only a few yards away) that there was now a group of protestors around Dr Paisley's car, and that there were heated exchanges going on as he reached the car, with Ian Junior seemingly taking a fair bit of the 'heat'. When they got inside, these exchanges continued through partly lowered windows. Things seemed to be escalating quite quickly.

Again, I was taken aback at the levels of anger being directed towards the Paisleys, which (from what I could hear)

58

appeared to be focused on them walking about the harbour accompanied by people from "Sinn Fein/IRA". As our driver started the bus, though, the group (which could by now be more accurately be described as an angry mob) turned its attention our way.

Our driver made a worried sound (something along the lines of "Oh shit") and started to move the bus, just as the mob started to close around us, with some very angry gestures and catcalls directed our way. Ahead, some vehicles, including a forklift truck, also appeared to be moving to block our route out of the car park, and some missiles were launched in our direction. I was now really quite concerned (in truth, I was terrified) and was mightily relieved when the driver made it (at high speed, and through the tiniest of gaps) out onto the road and away.

While we were now safe, I was (perhaps to my discredit) only slightly concerned for the Clerk. In my estimation, he was with police officers whose entire job was to provide protection for their 'principal', and I had no doubt they would have the tools to extricate Dr Paisley, and the other passengers, from the situation they were in.

The general mood on our bus was one of relief, and some nervous, but light-hearted, comments began to flow among the members. Might this, in fact, turn out to be a 'bonding' exercise, and might our Unionist members get a sense of their Nationalist colleagues' experiences with confrontational loyalism? I have to admit that those thoughts only occurred to me after the event, when we also found out that the mob had been around forty strong and that two arrests had been made.

At the time, I was just glad we were going to be able to continue the trip and that the bus was still fully glazed, if a little eggy. Despite the anxiety, my being in close proximity to all that fine fresh fish had given me an appetite, and I was happy that lunch had been arranged for our next stop.

The BBC crew followed our bus and eventually we met up with the Doc's car, with us all boarding the small ferry to sail across Strangford Lough. I thought that Dr Paisley must have been shaken by the reception he had received, but he didn't let it show. On the ferry, Martin Cassidy and his team continued to try to get 'the money shot' of the DUP's and Sinn Fein's togetherness (to no avail) and we disembarked and made the (thankfully uneventful) journey to Ardglass.

There the Committee met more fishermen at another harbour, then moved on to the local golf club, where lunch with local fishing dignitaries had been arranged. Word had obviously got out about the mob protest in Portavogie, and the local police had changed their tune from being relaxed to being very much on their guard, and they were quite visible for the rest of our trip. There is, of course, a different demographic in Ardglass and Kilkeel to that of Portavogie, and I didn't, frankly, expect there to be any more bother on this side of the Lough.

We arrived to find place names set out on two tables in a private room in the golf club restaurant, and the Clerk immediately spotted that Francie Molloy's name card was sitting just across from Dr Paisley's at the same table, which he knew would cause an issue. He quickly made a discreet request to the restaurant staff, and Francie's card was switched for another. This was done very subtly and as far as I know Francie was never aware of the change. Once more, Martin Cassidy had been thwarted!

On the plus side for the BBC, I think I recall that Dr Paisley asked for extra places to be set for Martin and his crew, and we were certainly content that there was no reason the Assembly couldn't pick up the bill for this on the Committee's behalf.

Before lunch was served, though, Dr Paisley called a formal meeting of the meeting, as there was some technical business (including matters relating to the upcoming inquiry which couldn't wait) that would otherwise have been addressed at the normal Friday meeting. I was unsure about this move at first, but the Clerk assured me that there was nothing to stop the Chairman doing this, or indeed to stop the Committee meeting formally wherever it pleased.

The business was swiftly attended to (and recorded diligently by Stephen and me) after which lunch was served. I'm pretty sure we had some fabulous locally caught fish and chips for lunch that day, and maybe some crab or prawns for our starter. At least I hope that was the case, given the reason for and location of the trip!

With everyone very well sated, we clambered back into our respective vehicles and made our way to the last stop of the day, in Kilkeel, where we were met by Alan McCulla, of the ANIFPO, and some of his team (as well as yet more local fishermen). I think the BBC crew called it a day at that point, never, I believe, managing to get their 'together' shot, but I'm sure they had some interesting footage from Portavogie, nonetheless.

After some meetings, and more walking around yet another harbour looking interested, we were taken inside a meeting hall, where I think there was a slightly raised stage which had a screen set up at the back. On this stage sat the local top fishing folk and the Chairman and Deputy Chairman of the Committee, all of whom were in prime position to watch the FPO's presentation on the screen. The rest of us were on the lower level in the hall.

In fairness, the room was very warm, the day had been long and full of incident, and we had partaken of a very filling lunch, but it wasn't long before I realized that Dr Paisley's eyes were closing over, and soon he was quite clearly asleep with, as I've heard it described, his 'head in his top pocket'.

The Clerk and I caught each other's eyes but neither of us was in a position to do anything about it, since we were not on the stage with the dignitaries. The FPO was giving an extremely earnest (and in their view important) presentation, and my embarrassment grew for the Chairman, and for how his apparent lack of interest might be perceived and reflect badly on the Committee. But fortunately, the cavalry arrived in the shape of George Savage who was sitting next to the Chairman, and who had also seen what was going on.

62

In a very good impersonation of a teenage boy sitting in a cinema next to his first date, George stretched his arms, then reached round the Chairman's back, tapping him briskly on his shoulder before retracting. It worked. The Chairman opened his eyes as if they were merely being rested and he nodded sagely at the most recent point. Then, somewhat amazingly, but true to usual form, he managed to ask a pertinent question. Potential crisis averted, and, I thought, an interesting insight into George's attitude towards a man who was, of course, a political opponent, but who (I assumed) may also in some sense have been a bit of a hero.

The meeting soon broke up and we were all taken back to Parliament Buildings without any further mishap. All in all, the consensus was that the day had been a success, in that the Committee's objectives had been met. However, given my brief exposure to the harsh realities of the mob's apparent rejection of one aspect of the democratically agreed process, I wasn't that keen on the Committee taking further trips away from Parliament Buildings in the near future.

It must have been a difficult trip for the Paisleys too, being given such a hard time by those they could normally have counted on as staunch supporters. The press later reported that Ian Junior had been forthright in his arguments with some of the more vocal women present, his line being that he and his father were working to try to save their husbands' jobs and that they wouldn't let the involvement of Sinn Fein stop them from doing that.

All in all, I was sure that the day had been a pretty good sounding board for Dr Paisley as to the potential political price of his involvement in the institutions that he continued to rail against. Would this change the way he chaired our Committee? I was both nervous, and excited, to find out.

Chapter 10: Supermarkets in the Senate – and it's the Dr Paisley show

The week after the fishing villages visit was probably the most hectic so far. Not only were we preparing for what we expected would be a major showdown between the Committee and the big retailers as part of the Inquiry into debt, but the FPOs had done such a good job of lobbying the Committee that the Chairman was minded to ask officials to attend an additional meeting to discuss the Cod Recovery Plan. This seemed all the more urgent since, as part of that Plan, the Irish Sea Cod fishery was to be closed to the Northern Ireland fleet from the 14th of February.

I remember thinking at the time that this was exactly how the Committee system was supposed to work. A sectoral interest group had briefed/lobbied the Committee and given its side of their particular story, after which the Committee had sought the Department's views, and would now, perhaps, seek to influence the Department's policies on the strength of what had been learned. There was now an immediacy and topicality to the whole process that we had not been used to under direct rule.

So it was that an extra Committee meeting was held on Wednesday the 9th of February, with DARD officials Gerry Lavery (the Fisheries Grade 3) and Jim Prentice (Grade 7), both of whom I knew fairly well and who both would become very familiar with the presentation end of the Committee table over the next few months.

Through the Chairman's brief that I'd drafted, the Clerk was able to summarize the issues raised by the FPOs, and the Chairman passed this summary on to the members, but the Cod Recovery Plan was the main subject of that morning's session. I had also supplied my usual questions brief, and on this occasion, I probably supplied too many questions, as there were quite a few that had not been used by the time the officials left.

I stress again that I was not trying to drive any agenda for the Committee, but I knew members were now very interested and engaged in the topic, and I must have felt that the Department's advance paper had offered up several of what I called 'penalty kicks' for the Committee to 'shoot' at the officials.

This would typically happen when I identified internal inconsistencies in a paper, or unsubstantiated claims, and the like. To be fair, the officials writing these papers were, themselves, still getting to grips with the whole accountability requirement, and sometimes didn't think too hard (or have time to think too hard) before they committed certain things to paper.

When the officials left, and the Committee reviewed its discussions in private session, a few of the penalty kicks had not been taken and the Committee agreed that they should be packaged up and issued to the Department as further information now sought by the Committee. That was also starting to become standard practice.

While this would undoubtedly ensure that the Committee ended up better informed, I was concerned that such follow up (with the Committee having to consider the outcome at a future meeting) wasn't the most efficient way of working for either the Committee or the Department. I wondered if it might be better to try to ensure that the most crucial matters were dealt with first time, most of the time, and I promised myself I would give some thought about how that could be achieved.

Before the Wednesday meeting finished, the Committee discussed the set-up of the Senate Chamber in Parliament Buildings for the up-coming evidence session with seven of the major retailers in Northern Ireland. This was arranged for Friday the 11th of February.

Since the normal Committee meeting rooms were quite small, there was a general feeling that more important Committee evidence sessions (across all Committees) should be held somewhere where there was plenty of public seating, and where cameras were in place to record and transmit proceedings. Transmission at that time meant only to the internal system (to which the press also had access) but I think that news outlets could also access the feed or ask for the recordings from it. The Senate Chamber met those criteria, and the ARD Committee was going to be the first to use it for a major 'set-piece'.

As the upper house of an earlier bi-cameral Parliament of Northern Ireland, the Senate had sat in its own Chamber, which was rather ornate compared to the Assembly Chamber, which had previous been that Parliament's 'House of Commons'.

There was some very grand seating in the Senate – particularly the chair on which the Senate Speaker would have sat, as recently as 1972, and the Assembly authorities were reluctant to interfere with those chairs, given their historical significance. There were also dispatch boxes and bench seating for Senators and it was actually quite hard to envisage how a Committee meeting could take place in that environment.

Dr Paisley was adamant that he would not be using the Speaker's Chair for the up-coming evidence session, as it was almost throne-like and would appear excessively formal. I expect he wasn't keen on how it would look to the public if he perched himself on such a throne.

Dr Paisley secured the Committee's agreement that he should write to the Assembly Speaker to ask that a more conventional Committee set-up be provided. There wasn't much time, so that was first business for the clerking team when the meeting ended.

I should mention that the Gentlemen's toilets immediately outside the Senate Chamber were the most fabulous and the grandest toilets I have ever seen (or am likely to see). They were huge (a small ballroom came to mind) and finished in sharp black and white tiling with the very best and whitest sanitary ware I have ever had the pleasure to wee in. Unfortunately, these toilets were later remodeled and reduced in size, to provide additional office space, and I remember being desperately disappointed when I saw this during a visit back to Parliament buildings long after my Committee years. I wished I'd taken photos of the 'before', although that might have seemed a little weird!

Friday the 11th came around very quickly, and the Clerking team went to view the Senate Chamber first thing. The Speaker had (I think reluctantly) agreed to the Chairman's request and some normal chairs and microphones had been provided. The layout, while it looked somewhat awkward, appeared to provide enough room between the front benches and the central table for the Chairman, Clerk, members and those giving their evidence to fit.

There was a 'full house' of members in attendance that morning, and the mood seemed very business-like. But there was also an undercurrent of uncertainty, since it was being widely reported (and expected) that the Assembly was going to be suspended later that day, principally because the International Commission on Decommissioning had recently reported that it had "received no information from the IRA as to when decommissioning will start"[13].

---

[13] Source: NI Assembly Website: General information – History of the Assembly

In a depressingly downward spiral over the previous 8 or 9 days, the Secretary of State had (with the aim of stopping the threatened resignation of the First Minister) threatened to suspend the Assembly if the IRA did not decommission. The IRA had responded with a statement that it had entered into no agreements to decommission arms, while the Continuity IRA claimed responsibility for a bomb in County Fermanagh at the start of that week[14].

Despite all this bad news, the Chairman and the members were intent on carrying out the planned business, and they agreed their tactics in closed session before the retailers were allowed in.

Almost all of the seven retailers had sent explanatory papers to the Committee in advance of the meeting, but many of these were only received in the last couple of days before the evidence session, meaning the Clerk and I had little time to prepare anything other than fairly basic questions.

The Clerk did, however, convince the Chairman (who in turn convinced the Committee) that it would be worth trying to operate a structured system for questions, through which individual retailers would be probed on their potato businesses immediately after each presentation, while wider procurement issues were to be probed in an open forum after individual Q&As were complete.

---

[14] Source: news.bbc.co.uk – 'Northern Ireland Chronology: 2000'

The Committee agreed that a couple of members would be assigned to 'grill' each retailer's team, with the first (the Co-operative Workers Society, better known as the Co-Op) to be questioned by the Chair and Deputy Chair. There seemed to be no hangover from last week's visit, and the Sinn Finn members were given their allocation like everyone else.

The Committee was also in receipt of a paper on agricultural produce prices that had been provided by the Assembly's own research service. I think the Clerk must have suggested that this paper was produced, as I wasn't really up to speed at that time on what the research service could offer. But it did strike me that here was a very credible resource made up of well-qualified staff, dedicated to providing members with information. I felt that the Committee team should seek to engineer as much use of that resource as possible, primarily because anything the Research Service could provide was something that the Committee team (and particularly I) wouldn't have to.

I'm not quite sure how the subject of potatoes had grown to such a level of importance since the Inquiry had been launched, but it may have been down to the quality (and volume) of lobbying about the potato sector that the Committee had received.

In any event, the retailers seemed well prepared to engage on this aspect, since representatives from two potato packing companies had joined 'their' retailers' teams. One (Wilson's Country) was involved with both Tesco and M&S while another (Glens of Antrim Potatoes) accompanied the Sainsburys team.

I had met Charlie McKillop from Glens of Antrim in my Rural Development days, when he had given the Rural Area Coordinator and me the full tour round his potato packing business. He had then given us his pitch on what he could do, and how many he could employ, if he received a grant from us. Unfortunately, we had to sheepishly tell him that we couldn't fund the private sector under the Programme at that time. I didn't expect him to remember me, but he seemed to (albeit not very fondly, given that we provided no help), and we had a brief word before things began.

The Chairman opened up the public session and it was clear from his tone that he wanted this to be seen as his show.

He started by referring to the research paper which, he said, had come from a "top Assembly researcher"[15]. Dr Paisley then went on to speak of the "catastrophe" that farmers were suffering from, the "terrible tragedy" of farmers shooting worthless bull calves that he had (apparently) seen on a farm visit the previous day, and then claim that when he'd asked the 'middlemen' whether they (like farmers) had gone bankrupt or considered suicide, they had "laughed and said 'No'".

---

[15]See minutes of evidence from 11 February 2000 as reproduced in the Committee's report: 'Retailing in Northern Ireland – A fair Deal for the Farmer?'

Such exaggeration, hyperbole and apocryphal storytelling was by now becoming quite familiar to us as Dr Paisley's standard way of operating, particularly in front of cameras and an audience. While he presumably intended this approach to provide credibility and gravity to the day's discussions, I was not convinced it did, as it was all a bit dramatic and obvious.

Dr Paisley also insisted on referring to "the housewife" throughout the session (for example, that "the housewife complains that she still pays as much" for foodstuff from supermarkets). He also gave a near-sermon on women going to work (as a reason for a change in purchasing and eating habits).

Even in those earliest days of the twenty-first century there was a general move away from the use of such overtly sexist (or perhaps you could call it old-fashioned) terminology, but that didn't appear to have been on Dr Paisley's radar at that point, which was interesting, but perhaps not unexpected at his age. He most definitely came across as 'old-school' when it came to matters domestic.

More interesting still (and telling) was the Chairman's defensive response when teething problems with the Senate's set-up reared their head early in the session.

The first retailer's representatives stood to make their presentation and had trouble making themselves heard (to both members and to those listening through the microphone system) and Dr Paisley went straight in with a number of disclaimers: "the Speaker made this arrangement", "we would have arranged things differently" and went on to say that the "microphones are not as good as the Speaker told us they were". Dr Paisley even suggested that the representatives should "give him an earful" about it.

While these were delivered in quite a humorous way, I found them a bit unnecessary. Were these people really about to hold the Chairman personally responsible for a few things going wrong? I doubted it, and I wasn't at all convinced that the Speaker would be delighted if he discovered that he'd been referred to in this way.

A quick and quiet word from the IT folk who'd set up the Chamber informed us that people needed to be seated to make their presentations for the mikes to pick them up, and, after the Chairman passed this on to the retailers, there were no further issues, and, happily, no subsequent need for the Speaker's ear to be filled.

Because the proceedings were being recorded by Hansard staff, I was able to relax a little more than usual, and I found the day's exchanges with the retailers quite instructive to me in building on my early assessments of the capabilities and personalities of some of the Committee's members. This might seem judgemental on my part, but it was important for me to better understand the people I was dealing with, and to help gauge how much support members might need.

Despite his sexism, hype and problem disclaimers, I felt that Dr Paisley provided quite a witty commentary as he (very effectively) compéred the proceedings. For example, when the representative from Musgrave Supervalu Centra (which served small owner-operated stores) attacked the larger retailers for their "massive stores" and "predatory pricing", Dr Paisley told him he'd be "lucky to get out with your head on your body." He went on to say that he was sorry that he did not "have the sword of a serjeant at arms" (presumably with which to protect the man rather than remove his head on the major retailers' behalf).

This approach worked well and kept the session quite light and good-natured. There was also some perceptible 'squirming' from the bigger retailers as Dr Paisley was clearly 'rooting for the underdog' and the MSC representative's points gained his and other members' support.

George Savage's contributions nearly all came from a standpoint that we'd heard already in the earlier meetings: to the effect that everyone else in the supply chain was making a living off the backs of the farmers. That came across as his unshakeable belief. George also tended to use a 'scattergun' approach and ask several (sometimes unrelated) questions at once. This could allow the respondent to concentrate on an answer that caused them least discomfort, and George rarely followed up on the unanswered ones.

Gardiner Kane made no attempt to hide the fact that he was reading from pre-prepared questions. This was not really an issue until he repeated (verbatim to the second retailer's representatives) a question that the Chairman had asked of the first. That turned out not to be a unique occurrence for Gardiner and the funniest (though embarrassing at the time) example (occurring some months later) was when another member repeated the first member's question to one of the Department's officials (which was bad enough) only for Gardiner to come in and ask the exact same question for a third time!

Gerry McHugh was also fond of asking multiple questions at once, and on this day, he seemed to bring in subjects unconnected to the purpose of this meeting. This sometimes happened with Gerry, who I thought also had a tendency to say too much when putting his questions, with his delivery also being a bit monotone. I found that when I took the time to read his contributions in the Official Report, I could quite often see what Gerry was getting at, and indeed the validity of some of what he was trying to say or to establish, but all too often the meaning was lost in his delivery.

Boyd Douglas' line of questioning seemed to be influenced and motivated by his personal experience as a farmer (e.g., the poor price he had been offered for "good potatoes") rather than a strategic level consideration. Fair enough, perhaps, but it occurs to me now that he (and others) should have declared such interests at the start of the session (not least for the benefit of those taking members' questions).

I think we took the view early in the Committee's existence that members' original declaration of interests was enough. That would change in future meetings, with the Clerk frequently suggesting to the Chair that interests in the day's specific subject matter should be declared and recorded.

When it came to Billy Armstrong's turn, he made an attempt to interpret figures that the Committee had just been given in the research paper, asserting (in a critical manner) that only 7% of one supermarket's potatoes came from Northern Ireland. While a figure of 7% was mentioned in the paper, I could see that it did not mean what he said it meant, and his contribution caused some confusion.

Billy always had time to talk to you, and was very personable, but I was afraid that this episode (together with some earlier contributions) might be damaging in terms of his credibility with the other Committee members.

Ian Paisley Junior, on the other hand, correctly identified relevant figures from the papers and challenged the retailers coherently on the price differentials that those figures showed. I found that Junior sometimes enjoyed mischief-making in the Committee and winding up some other members. But, when he wasn't doing that, I thought he could be very adept at performing the Committee's challenge function.

PJ Bradley demonstrated a willingness to take on a major and potentially controversial issue when he sought assurances from the retailers that a pricing 'cartel' didn't exist among them (as had been alleged by farmers). I thought that PJ's line of approach, in which he didn't make any grandstanding allegations himself but simply allowed the retailers to address others' allegations objectively, was a good one and demonstrated an astuteness on his part.

Individually, members all got their turn, but I thought that they weren't yet acting as a collective. I must acknowledge that the time for questions to each retailer was limited, but I got no real sense of the retailers' responses being picked up and influencing what many of the members said next or enabling deeper exploration of a particular point.

It must have been particularly frustrating to the retailers that, despite every single one of them reporting that their retail prices (for potatoes at least) had fallen by 50% over the past 9-10 months, member after member kept insisting that they 'knew' that retail prices for potatoes and other foods were constantly rising. Similarly, despite all the retailers stressing that it made commercial sense to use locally produced potatoes rather than importing them, except where certain varieties were not locally grown, or were grown only seasonally, members insisted that it "was known" that there were "big numbers of potatoes" coming into Northern Ireland.

It seemed that some of the members weren't really that keen on listening, and simply wanted to grind their own particular 'axe'. I remember feeling quite frustrated by this on the day. Still, there was plenty of information being supplied, including some interesting 'nuggets' (e.g., when it was explained, in response to John Dallat's complaint, that 'Ayrshire milk' was made in Northern Ireland under licence rather than being imported).

All the exchanges were being recorded as 'Minutes of Evidence' by the Official Report so I felt somewhat reassured that the Committee's Inquiry report could (and should) at least accurately reflect the evidence that was being heard, and I was determined that would be the case.

After a fairly long session (which was well time-managed by the Chairman) the retailers left, and the Committee again went into private session. Members conducted a few more items of business, after which the Chairman brought the meeting to a close. In light of the uncertainty about the Assembly's suspension, the Committee agreed not to set a date for its next meeting, and it was left that the Chairman would call the next meeting only when it was appropriate to do so.

I will never forget following Dr Paisley (and Ian Junior) out of the Senate Chamber, past the ballroom-like toilets, and along the corridor into the Great Hall after the meeting, as there were journalists, MLAs and staff milling about everywhere. The place was 'hiving'.

It seemed that the word on the street was that a suspension was now inevitable, and the journalists were scrambling for views from senior politicians. As he barged through the melee, Dr Paisley was asked to comment on the anticipated suspension. In his usual fashion, he didn't break stride as he roared his response which was something like "It is terrible; it's an absolute tragedy".

I was, again, quite taken aback by this. Dr Paisley and his party were clearly not fans of the Institutions or of the Good Friday Agreement that had led to their formation. He and his party colleagues had been (and continued to be) very vociferous on that point, and on the decommissioning issue.

But I got the sense, in that moment, of Dr Paisley's internal conflict around his involvement with the Committee. I felt that this unprepared response said much more about the good that he genuinely felt that he and his Committee could do for an agri-food industry that was very close to his heart, and which was (by all accounts) struggling. Add the fact that his Committee's inquiry had got underway with a very public and successful 'Dr Paisley show' and it must really have frustrated him (at least on one level) that it now looked like the Inquiry was going to be stalled.

Sure enough, later that day the Secretary of State, Peter Mandelson, signed an Order, under legislative powers from the Northern Ireland Act 2000, suspending the Assembly and restoring Direct Rule.

I had only been 'up the hill' for eleven or twelve weeks. What was now in store for the Assembly, for its Committees and for its staff?

I too was frustrated and disappointed by the suspension, not least because I believed I had seen some 'green shoots' of proper parliamentary and inclusive politics, rather than the tribal and divisive politics that were all I had ever known.

Would these shoots ever get the chance to grow?

Chapter 11: Everyone takes a breath

It was a very strange atmosphere in the office on the following Monday morning. There was an element of relief that the treadmill had stopped, but also a real concern that it might not restart any time soon, and a fear of what the wider consequences of that might be for the Assembly, for its staff, and for Northern Ireland as a whole.

Pretty soon (indeed, in the first week of suspension) the IRA withdrew its co-operation with the Commission on Decommissioning, and we looked to be in for the long haul, politically.

It was very pleasant being able to take time to have tea and lunch breaks and to work normal, sensible, hours. Those had been the stuff of dreams since I had gone 'up the hill', and I certainly took advantage of our new-found freedom and insisted that Stephen did too.

But it also concerned me that the Committee had amassed a lot of material from the various evidence sessions already held and I felt that we as a Committee team should be as prepared as we possibly could be for the Assembly's potential reinstatement, and the recommencement of Committee business.

With the Clerk's agreement, I therefore decided to make a start on 'writing up' the Committee's Inquiry so far and drafting conclusions and recommendations for the

Committee's consideration on its return. I only felt confident enough to take this work on because the Clerk had already indicated his appreciation of my writing abilities, calling me an "excellent draftsman". The Clerk was also delighted as it meant that he didn't have to do the work.

I had previously drafted policy papers in the Department, and recommendations for direct rule Ministers, but this was very different. I thought it a fundamental requirement that the Committee's conclusions and recommendations had to be supported by the evidence. The biggest issue I had was that while members would need to 'own' the draft report, it was clear that some of their oft-repeated views were not supported by the evidence they had heard.

What made the task even harder was the fact that my draft report needed to be acceptable to, and endorsed by, such a wide spectrum of members, who were coming from opposing sides of a political divide, and when there were even significant differences among those from the same 'side'.

Some members also hailed from the Minister's party, which made it difficult to be overly critical of the Minister, or to recommend radical actions by the Department to which the Minister might object. Nor (I was finding) did members think like Civil Servants, who had been my previous 'customers'. I definitely had a job on my hands.

So, my next few weeks were spent between relaxing in the basement canteen (which was still frequented by MLAs, and which offered very good food at very affordable prices), taking part in Committee-wide reviews of how things had gone and what might be done better, and being buried among the minutes of evidence and submissions from the various groups involved in the Inquiry. There was virtually no contact with Dr Paisley or the other members – effectively the Committee did not exist.

After those few weeks, I presented a draft report to the Clerk, with the snappy (I must have thought) title of 'Retailing in Northern Ireland – A Fair deal for the Farmer?' The title was meant to play on farmers' representatives' insistence that all they really wanted was a fair deal.

All in all, I was quite pleased with the fruits of my labour, and so was the Clerk, but I was also struck by the amount of time and effort that it had taken for me to sift through all the evidence.

There had been some slight change to the political 'mood music' as early as March 2000, and there must have been huge efforts going on behind the scenes to try to rescue the Institutions.

The crux was now about whether there would be 'prior decommissioning' of the IRA's weapons (i.e., that this would be carried out before the Assembly could be restored). The First Minister, David Trimble, had indicated that he might be prepared to return without it, provided decommissioning was in fact dealt with, and over the next couple of months he faced down very significant opposition from within his own Party on this issue.

As usual, careful choreography was deployed and this included a statement from the IRA that it was ready to begin a process that would "completely and verifiably" put its arms beyond use[16], along with a suggestion that international figures would inspect IRA arms dumps and confirm that they were not being used. The Secretary of State did his bit by announcing that he would restore the Assembly and, at midnight on 29 May 2000, power was restored to Stormont.

It had been just over three months, but it hadn't felt that long, and we could feel the treadmill powering up under our collective feet.

---

[16] Source: news.bbc.co.uk – 'Northern Ireland Chronology: 2000'

Chapter 12: Back in harness and raring to go

The Committee met again on the 2nd of June 2000. There were still just the three of us in the Committee support team (and Martin was still Clerking two Committees), despite there having been some talk of additional staff being sourced to help us out.

Members had to get used to a couple of changes to our procedures. For example, Stephen and I were now recording, for the minutes of proceedings, the timings of members' comings and goings in the Committee meetings.

This was, I think, one of the Committee-wide improvements that had been discussed during the period of suspension, and I think it stemmed from some members being uncomfortable with having their names associated with decisions made in their absence. Members quite frequently dipped in and out of meetings to attend to other business, and it seemed reasonable to want to be able to determine who exactly was present when a Committee line or decision was agreed.

The Clerk and I had to be constantly 'on the ball' in order to alert the Chairman if the Committee's quorum of five members was in danger of being lost, and the recorded attendance timings also helped demonstrate that the Committee was quorate as it conducted its business.

Just before the Committee's return, Martin and I had considered how best to utilize the draft report that I had already prepared. Martin then (with Dr Paisley's approval) allowed me to take the lead in talking the Committee through three options as to how they might proceed with the Inquiry that had already begun. All these options would, in one form or another, utilize the work I had done, and which I wasn't going to let go to waste.

The summer was approaching, and, despite the three-month suspension, there was an expectation that the Assembly would still take its full summer recess. The option that I pushed for hardest, and which was agreed by the Chairman and members at the first meeting back, was to publish an interim report on the retailing issues before summer recess, with two further reports planned for the Autumn, covering the pig and beef sectors.

There were still several evidence sessions outstanding that would cover these two sectors, and these were hastily re-arranged by the team, starting with another Senate Chamber 'set piece' at the next meeting on the 9th of June. The Chairman was still not entirely happy with the practical set up in the Chamber, but we made do. In this session, five further organisations had the opportunity to make presentations and answer members' questions.

Although Martin had every confidence in the work I had done on the retailers' evidence, he was conscious that neither he nor I had any expertise in retailing or marketing (my six years as a warehouseman in Marks and Sparks notwithstanding). He therefore suggested to Dr Paisley that the Committee might appoint a Specialist Advisor to consider the draft report against the evidence taken.

I could have been miffed at the thought of this, but it was a very sensible approach in the circumstances. With the Chairman's endorsement of the idea, the Committee agreed to it, and that day appointed an advisor that had been identified (with the help of the Assembly's Research Service) as having retail expertise and being suitable for the task.

Between the 9th of June meeting and the Committee's next meeting on the 22nd, the Committee team got an extra pair of hands by way of an Agency appointment to the role of clerical support. I believe that a few agency staff were taken on for several Committees at the same time and we secured the services of a young man called Easton for our Committee. We had plenty for him to do.

In fairly short order, the Specialist Advisor considered and endorsed the work I had done on the retailers' report, offering a few minor suggestions and enhancements, with Martin also suggesting some helpful additions to my conclusions section. The next few meetings were then spent going through the (amended) draft report line by line agreeing, or amending then agreeing, each and every paragraph.

The Committee engaged well and worked hard on this process and were kept well on track by the Chairman (and the Clerk) while doing so. The Committee met four times in the space of six days (once in the Stormont hotel where Committee members were attending an event, with only the Clerk present from our team).

On a couple of occasions, the Committee worked through lunchtime. When this happened, we arranged for lunch to be provided by the Assembly's catering team out of our Committee budget and it was really top-notch grub. We felt it only fair (and thankfully Dr Paisley agreed) that we order enough for both members and Committee staff! In time, I quite looked forward to such occasions.

By the 27th of June, the Committee had agreed the contents of the report, including an Executive Summary which I'd also drafted, and formally agreed to its publication, and to the inclusion of the minutes of evidence ('Hansards') relating to the report.

It was then down to staff to work with colleagues from the Stationery Office (TSO, who maintained an office in Parliament Buildings at that time) to produce the physical printed report. I was in no way credited as the author of the report, as ownership had been taken by the Committee, but it was very satisfying on a personal level to see my work in print.

The report was launched in a blaze of publicity (actually it was a minor flicker of a press release) at the start of July. It seemed odd to me at the time that Dr Paisley didn't demand a much higher profile launch, but I suppose there was a balance to be struck for him between taking credit for the Committee's work, and criticism for his working with Sinn Fein on that Committee.

There were two further Committee meetings ahead of the summer recess, and in the first of these, the Committee took yet more evidence which would feed into their proposed reports on the pig and beef sectors.

This took place again in the Senate Chamber, where members continued to find difficulty in organizing their papers, since they had no tables in front of them on the bench seating. This was becoming an issue (and it was really displeasing to the Chairman) and the Committee agreed that the Speaker should again be approached and asked to sort it out.

During the early part of the Committee's meeting of the 30th of June (in the Committee room, before members moved to the Senate Chamber), a situation arose regarding members' interests, which I found interesting, and which required the Chairman to make a 'ruling'.

The Minister had sought the Committee's views and advice on the allocation of additional milk quota. When this item was reached on the agenda, three members (Billy Armstrong, Boyd Douglas and Gerry McHugh) declared an interest, since they were milk producers and therefore potential beneficiaries of the Minister's decision. The three contributed to discussions, but then absented themselves from the Committee's final decision-making on the subject.

A Committee motion was proposed, suggesting that quota would be allocated among all active producers, and an amendment was also proposed (by the two SDLP members) that it should be allocated only to full time farmers in Less Favoured Areas (LFAs). Presumably this reflected what their Party colleague, the Minister, wanted to see happen.

In the absence of the three 'declared interest' members, five were left to vote on the motions by a show of hands. On the amendment, there was a tie (2:2) meaning that the amendment fell. The motion was then voted on and it too was a 2:2 tie, meaning that the motion fell too. In neither case did the Chairman use what would have effectively been a casting vote.

In the absence of agreement, all the Committee was able to do was to agree that a summary of the Committee's deliberations be passed to the Minister.

While most onlookers would probably agree that it had been the right for the three members to absent themselves, their withdrawal left the Committee unable to reach a firm decision and give a definitive answer to the Minister. Furthermore, the three members were unable to fully represent their constituents on what was an important issue to the dairy sector. That didn't feel quite right to the team, or to the Committee members themselves.

The Chairman had not asked the members to withdraw from the meeting or refrain from voting. Indeed, under advice from the Clerk, he had ruled that they did not have to do either of those things, given that their interests had been properly declared and would be recorded in the minutes of proceedings.

It did seem to us to be a matter of some significance and wider relevance, and the events of the 30th of June meeting were reported to the Speaker via the Committee management structures. In a later sitting of the Assembly (25th of September 2000 during the debate on the Committee's first report) the Speaker gave his ruling[17] confirming that the Chairman's line had been correct, and that his approach should be applied to future meetings of all Committees, as well as proceedings in the Assembly Chamber.

The Speaker's endorsement of his approach, and insistence on its wider application to other Committees, would have pleased the Chairman no end, and I'm sure it also enhanced the Clerk's credibility with him and with the other Committee members.

The Committee's last meeting before summer recess took place on the 3rd of July and, according to the Minutes, I didn't attend that day. I have forgotten why, but I suspect that I may have had a holiday booked before I had joined the Assembly, and that my prior leave request had been honoured by my current management. In any event, I didn't miss much, as the

---

[17] Official Report Bound Volumes - Volume 6 page 164

Committee's decisions recorded in the minutes of that day's meeting were mainly to put things off until after recess.

June had been a really hectic month, so I was very glad of my holidays and of the recess in general. I was still very unsure about the future. While there had been some progress regarding the inspection of IRA weapons, and independent assurances that the weapons could not be used without detection, there was no certainty that decommissioning would occur and that things would settle down, politically.

Whatever might be ahead, though, the 1999/2000 Assembly session had demonstrated that working in the Assembly was no easy career option for me. The whole vibe surrounding the Assembly was so much more dynamic than I had experienced to date as a Civil Servant. Everything now was immediate where nothing had ever been immediate before.

There is no doubt that having locally elected Ministers and Committee office holders had changed the way that government worked in Northern Ireland. While this had meant a huge volume of work for the Committee team, with no sign of the workload letting up in any way, it was actually very exciting to be a part of.

For now, therefore, I was very happy to stick with it, and see what joys the next Assembly session would bring.

Part Two 2000/2001 - The Middle bit

Chapter 13: A new session, new staff and a mountain of evidence to climb

The Committee met on Tuesday the 29th of August 2000, and, somewhat strangely, this was still considered and recorded as being within the 1999/2000 session. I think that this was a slightly earlier Committee return from recess than we had hoped for, but we had recharged our batteries over the Summer, so we shrugged our shoulders and got on with it.

The first meeting in the 2000/2001 session then took place on the 8th of September, with an extremely busy agenda which included further evidence for the Inquiry and a briefing from the Permanent Secretary on a 'hot topic' issue of the exclusion of sheep from grazing on land surrounding the Silent Valley reservoir.

Preparations for this meeting were a little difficult. We had, over the Summer, lost our agency Clerical support staff member, Easton, who had, as I recall, decided he wanted to be a poet rather than an Assembly staff member. Fair play to him.

Crucially, we were also down our Executive Support staff member since Stephen had decided to return to his parent department. I can't fully recall his reasoning, but I'm sure it was in part linked to the continuing political uncertainty. I may also have had something to do with his decision.

My working relationship with Stephen had started out really well. I involved him in matters which would normally be above his pay grade and gave him plenty of positive feedback for his excellent work, which had included clever and workable solutions to some problems we had faced.

More recently, though, our relationship had become a little strained, after Stephen had taken significant offence at what I had thought was a throwaway comment.

To my mind, it was a classic case of offence perceived but not intended. He had asked me if he should carry out a particular task, or if I wanted to do it myself. Humorously (or so I thought) I answered, "sure why keep a dog and bark yourself?" By this I had meant that I was more than happy to delegate such a task to my staff, when they were more than capable of doing it.

Unfortunately, he perceived this as me calling him "a dog" and he became really angry, threatening to report me and to leave the Assembly secretariat there and then. I apologized profusely and tried to explain that I had no intention of offending him, but it took several days for him to calm down.

In truth, I never felt fully comfortable in my relationship with him after that, in case I should offend him again. That was a shame, because I had really liked the guy.

While I was certain that I would miss his excellent work as part of our team, and his willingness to accept responsibility for all sorts of tasks (to do some of the barking, as I'd probably have put it) I had to accept his decision to go.

We did secure the services of another clerical officer, although I can't quite recall if she was agency or another secondee from the Civil Service. In any event, Kyran (which may not be the correct spelling of her name) was now part of the team.

She would certainly be needed. There was already a massive amount of work to do, and then the Committee was advised, at the 8th of September meeting, that the Department was bringing forward two legislative Bills in the current session. The Committee would therefore need to set aside sufficient time for its statutory scrutiny of these Bills at Committee Stage, while at the same time concluding its Inquiry, producing two more reports, and dealing with its 'normal' day-to-day business.

I was very relieved when the Committee took the decision (at Martin's suggestion) to appoint another Specialist Advisor to assist with the Pigs and Beef sectors aspects of the Inquiry. That took some of the pressure off me, as I wasn't at all convinced that I could have done as good a job of sifting the piles of evidence relating to those sectors without the luxury of having a suspended Assembly and no committee meetings to arrange.

I was certainly no expert on those sectors either, although I had, as usual, fed some draft questions to members, based on the papers that were sent in by each of the organisations in advance of their giving evidence. The Chairman (and the Clerk) always ensured that some of the key questions were asked and answered during each session, in order that there was a sufficient evidence-base for the Committee's next two reports.

Dr Paisley also continued to punctuate his contributions with mildly sexist and even (we would now see as) mildly racist remarks (e.g., when evidence was given of Chinese people's taste for pork, he said "It's as well they are not Jews")[18]. It is only fair to stress, however, that no-one appeared to take any exception to his comments at the time.

I must also acknowledge that the Committee members appeared to be quite knowledgeable across the beef and pigs sectors. They seemed well able to follow all the presentations, and even to formulate their own follow-up questions, which was refreshing.

The Department had also given its formal response to the Retailer report, clearing the way for it to be brought before the Assembly, and the Committee agreed to seek an Assembly debate on it for Monday the 25th of September.

The next few meetings flew by, and included more evidence-taking for the Inquiry, as well as clause-by-clause consideration of the Dogs Bill, which had been introduced by the DARD Minister, and preparation for the introduction of a Fisheries (Amendment) Bill, which would cut across the

---

[18] Minutes of Evidence of the Agriculture and Rural Development Committee from 30 June 2000 (Ulster Pork and Bacon Forum, paragraph 281) as archived on the NI Assembly website

responsibilities of another Committee (Culture Arts and Leisure).

There was an interesting exchange at the 22nd of September meeting when PJ Bradley, as an SDLP member, reflected that a Committee press release following the previous meeting had used language stronger than he would have used. I don't recall exactly what was said, but I assume the language was critical of the SDLP Minister.

This was just the sort of thing that I'd feared might happen although the Clerk was, on this occasion, able to reply that the draft press release had been read out to, and agreed by, members who had been at the meeting (PJ had not).

It was an important principle that the Committee could, provided it had a quorum, agree a committee view on any matter, including the issue of a press release, and the Chairman wasted no time in pointing out that if members attended the meetings, they could influence such decisions.

Dr Paisley was able to say this from a position of relative strength regarding his own attendance. He had missed only one of the eighteen Committee meetings in the 1999/2000 session, and that had been due to House of Commons business. In fairness, the deputy Chairman, George Savage, had missed only two himself, making them both among the best attenders among the Committee's members.

Chapter 14: The 'Fair Deal' gets a fair wind in the Chamber

As requested by our members, the Assembly's Business Committee agreed to schedule a plenary debate on the Committee's 'Fair Deal' report on the 25th of September. This was the first Statutory Committee report to reach this stage, and again placed our Committee as 'trailblazers' within the Assembly. I am certain that the Chairman was more than happy with that outcome.

The concept of securing the Assembly's endorsement of the Committee's findings came, I think, from the Clerk's and others' study of how things were done in other legislatures (mainly Westminster). In any event, having such a debate certainly made sense in terms of the report's credibility and the Committee members' expectation that something might actually come of it.

The motion itself had been agreed by the Committee but was tabled in the names of the Chairman and Deputy Chairman. The motion was quite long, but essentially it asked the Assembly to endorse the report and to urge the Minister (and others) to implement the report's sixteen recommendations. The Assembly debate began shortly after 4pm after plenty of other plenary business and Question Time had been completed.

The debate on a Committee report was a whole new experience for the Clerking team too. It meant us (my recollection is that it was just the Clerk and me) taking our seats in the Officials' Box, which was another exciting first.

There was one of these 'boxes' on either side of the chamber. Each had its own entrance from the corridor at the back of the Chamber, but the entrance to ours was not to be confused with the one beside it, which was used by the Speaker and the 'Clerks at Table' and led only to their seats. Going in the wrong door was not a mistake you wanted to make in the middle of an Assembly sitting!

The Box doesn't have direct access to the Floor of the Assembly Chamber, which is, quite rightly, considered to be the habitat of elected MLAs only, but its proximity to the Floor did make it possible for us to follow very closely the tenor of debate and to arrange for the passing of notes to the Chairman as the debate went on.

Of course, the DUP, at that time, was not the largest Unionist party, and it was the members of the Ulster Unionist Party who sat closest to the Speaker's chair (and therefore the Officials' box). Dr Paisley's DUP front bench seat (from where he would deliver his speech) was a fair distance from the Box. We therefore had to arrange (with Dr Paisley) for a 'runner' (I don't recall who, but it was a Party 'back-bencher' who wasn't a committee member) to act as a go-between if we needed to be in contact with the Chairman, or him with us.

The Minister was in the Chamber for the debate, as was expected, given that her office was referred to in the motion, and her officials took up residence in the Officials' box on the other side of the Chamber. SDLP MLAs sat closest to the Box on that side.

Given that this was a Committee motion, it fell to the Clerk to provide some 'bullet point' speaking notes for the Chair's and Deputy Chair's contributions, since they were the Committee's office holders and would therefore speak on behalf of the Committee.

Other members were free to bring their own thoughts to the debate, but the Chairman had made his expectation very clear that everyone would speak in support of the motion, given that the Committee had considered and agreed every last paragraph, sentence and word of it.

The debate itself[19] was fairly uneventful. In moving the motion, and speaking first, the Chairman did not waste the opportunity to highlight the report's, the Committee's, and especially his own, importance, with plenty of hyperbole to the fore (with his description of "disaster" for the industry, and the "suicide" anecdote once again being trotted out). His contribution appeared very much to be his own, rather than drawing very much on what we'd provided. We had no issue with that, and nor were we surprised by it.

---

[19] Reported in the Official Report Bound Volume 6 pages 151-166

The Deputy Chairman's contribution came next, and it appeared to (mainly) follow the prepared materials. I say mainly, since George confusingly (but typically) threw in a couple of unrelated issues that were important to him, presumably because the Minister was in the Chamber and therefore 'fair game' for a George attack.

The next three Committee members said nothing unexpected, with PJ Bradley emphasizing his Ministerial colleague's actions to date, Gardiner Kane giving his own view on a co-operation issue, rather than that which appeared in the report, and Gerry McHugh continuing to peddle the 'increasing prices in the shops' myth, while (as we'd also come to expect from Gerry) promoting a North/South approach and a move away from a dependence on British policies.

Kieran McCarthy, from the Alliance party, spoke on behalf of David Ford, who hadn't been able to make the debate, and Kieran mentioned that the Northern Ireland Forum (a forerunner to this Assembly) had also brought out a report on the same subject, to which he had been a party.

This surprised me, since I knew nothing about the Forum, nor about any work it might have done. In truth, I'd paid very little attention at all to local political matters before my journey up the hill, but on hearing this news, I resolved to take a look at the Forum's report out of personal interest when I got the chance.

John Dallat emphasized the Committee's collective responsibility for producing the report, highlighting that it had been a collective response from people with quite diverse political perspectives. I thought that this was a highly significant point, and I felt a surge of personal and professional satisfaction at having played such a significant role in facilitating such a collective response. These were still early days of our politicians working together and I was sure that this was exactly the sort of outcome that the authors of the peace process would have hoped for.

There were no other contributions from Committee members, although Ian Junior was granted an intervention during Willie McCrea's speech[20]. I thought it a strange decision for the party not to field another Committee member to contribute, but it seemed the DUP 'big guns' were sent out in support of the party leader's Chairmanship. The DUP's Jim Shannon (although I wasn't sure if he totally fitted the 'big gun' description) also said a few words.

The Minister's contribution built on John Dallat's, to the point of Brid Rodgers commending the Chairman for bringing all shades of political opinion together on the subject. I did an actual 'double take' in the box at that point, since their relations were still anything but warm.

Normal service was soon resumed, however, when the Minister took issue with someone's behaviour on the DUP

---

[20] It is customary to ask: "will the Member give way?" if an MLA wants to contribute while another 'has the floor'. There is no requirement to give way and allow an intervention, but Members often do to enhance debate.

benches and Dr Paisley angrily assumed that she was referring to him (which she then denied). That was much better sport!

The Minister's welcome for the report was more general than specific, and she claimed that many of the report's recommendations directed at her Department were "in progress" or that the 'Vision Group' for Agriculture, which she had recently appointed, would come up with its own solutions on the matters covered by the recommendations. That probably explained the Minister's 'buttering up' of Dr Paisley's performance at the start of her speech, I thought.

Whether or not we passed any notes to Dr Paisley (I think not, as it was really hard to keep up with the debate, hand-write notes and get them delivered to him) he didn't miss this point. In summing up the debate, the Chairman expressed his concern that the Minister had not given any indication of how the Department would implement the relevant recommendations.

Dr Paisley went on to say that he wanted the Minister to "join the band, to come into step with what we have put before her". I thought this an amusing analogy to use, given that Ms. Rodgers was an outspoken critic of the Orange Order regarding its march in Portadown (Drumcree, Garvaghy Road, bands and all). That may or may not have been deliberate, but it was another interesting episode in the Paisley/Rodgers dynamic.

In any event, the Assembly agreed the motion without Division, and the report was duly endorsed. A good result for the Committee, and (in my not-quite-humble estimation) for me.

As a footnote, I did look up the report referred to by Kieran McCarthy. It had been prepared by Standing Committee D (Agriculture and Fisheries issues) of the Northern Ireland Forum for Political Dialogue. The report was entitled 'The Sourcing in Northern Ireland of Agricultural Produce by National Supermarkets and Retailers' and it had issued on the 23rd of January 1998, the Forum already having produced a report on potatoes issues.

The Standing Committee's report contained recommendations that were very, very similar to those in our Statutory Committee's report, and I remember having very mixed feelings about this. On the one hand, the similarities arguably added further credibility to the conclusions that I had brought forward, and the Committee had adopted, in 'our' report. On the other hand, however, it made me realize that this was ground that had already (and recently) been covered and that elected representatives may be unduly keen on familiar subjects.

It also demonstrated to me that such reports had a seriously short 'currency'. In truth, from my Department days, I already realized that reports like these generally sat gathering dust on departmental shelves, and if ignored long enough they would not effect any actual change.

My (I suppose naïve) faith in the practical importance of the work I was doing with the Committee was knocked slightly by seeing this 'doppelganger'(and already forgotten) report, but I still maintained a healthy confidence in the wider importance of the process.

Chapter 15: Tempers fray

For some members, I reckon there must have been too much 'sweetness and light' and mutual appreciation expressed during the debate on the retailing report, as the Committee's next Friday meeting (on the 29th of September) was much 'spikier' than usual.

Among the items on a long agenda, there was discussion about the Minister's response to the retailing report, and there was also a sense of urgency about concluding the evidence required to allow completion of the Pigs and Beef sectoral reports. It was as if they'd had enough of these subjects, and now wanted to move on. I concurred.

The Committee now also had much more business being generated by the Department, and the meeting included consideration of a draft Committee report on the Dogs (amendment) Bill.

The topic of the retailing report brought the meeting's first difficult moment. The Sinn Fein Committee members queried (fairly passively, I thought) the Chairman's actions in writing to the Permanent Secretary of the DHSSPS (to provide a copy of the Committee's report) rather than to that Department's (Sinn Fein) Minister.

Dr Paisley was not at all passive in his response, saying that everyone knew his Party's policy on Sinn Fein Ministers and that he wouldn't be changing his ways. He further asserted that while he had written the letter as Committee Chair, this did not imply the Committee's agreement to its contents.

I wasn't quite sure that I agreed with that assertion. Actually, I was quite sure that he was wrong, but the Clerk seemed to be letting this one go, and the querying members did not put up any counter argument, so I decided to keep my counsel. Sometimes I was very happy to be the Assistant Clerk, rather than the Clerk!

Unfortunately, that exchange set the tone for what then became quite a belligerent meeting, and things came to a real head when John Dallat proposed a motion for the Committee to take a specific action in relation to the Silent Valley reservoir sheep grazing ban.

Whether there was an actual party-political divide on the policy on this issue, or Ian Junior was just up to some mischief, I am not sure. In any event, Junior tabled an amendment to John's motion, which (if carried) would put the onus on John to raise the matter initially as an Assembly Question and, depending on the answer received, the Committee might then consider taking the matter up.

The vote on the amendment was run by the normal show of hands (sought and counted by the Clerk) with a 4:4 result meaning that Ian Junior's amendment fell. Or, rather, that it should have fallen.

I missed whatever non-verbal communication had taken place, but the Chairman seemed to wake up to the fact that his boy's amendment had just failed. So, he suddenly announced that he had, in fact, wanted to vote on this matter (bearing in mind that he hadn't previously exercised a casting vote) and he declared that the first vote was therefore null and void. He instructed the Clerk to take the vote again and, with the addition of his own vote, the amendment was carried.

John Dallat was incandescent, as you'd expect, and suggested that he'd be making a formal complaint about what he argued was a shocking abuse of position. Dr Paisley just smiled and shrugged his shoulders, as if to say, "bring it on".

The shock of what was (to us) such an obvious breach of procedure must have made the Clerk (and me sitting behind him) forget to advise on the next stage, which was for the amended motion to be then subject to approval by the Committee. That just didn't happen. Oops! Afterwards, we were concerned that this was all a bit of a procedural mess, and that it might reflect badly on us as advisors to the Committee.

Sure enough, John Dallat raised the matter with the Speaker as a Point of Order in the Plenary session on the 2nd of October. I was a little surprised at the outcome when the Speaker returned to the matter in Plenary on the 9th of October[21], but on reflection it made perfect sense.

---

[21] Official Report Bound Volume 6 – page 269

The Speaker referred to several instances in Standing Orders where the Chairman's role in Committee is effectively one of exercising the same powers as the Speaker, albeit in the context of managing Committee business. He felt that Chairs should also be responsible for upholding Standing Orders and that it would not, therefore, be proper for him to rule on matters that took place in Committees.

This cleverly avoided the avalanche of "he did, she didn't" stories and complaints from our and other Committees that the Speaker would inevitably have had to rule upon, and, while it arguably gave carte blanche for Chairs to run things as they pleased, the Speaker had clearly articulated the expectation that Chairs would uphold Standing Orders as they did so.

I might also speculate that Dr Paisley may have been on the end of some 'usual channels' contact from the Speaker's Office about his conduct of this particular vote. I wasn't a party to any such exchange, but this dubious practice was never repeated.

I remember being interested in the 'Point of Order' process that led to the Speaker's 'ruling' that he would not be ruling on this matter. Assembly Standing Orders already interested me, and I think this issue provided a 'spark' that would eventually lead me in a change of direction towards the procedural side of Assembly business.

For now, though, we were glad that no criticism had landed on the heads of Committee staff, but we could see that John Dallat remained pretty sore about the whole thing.

One other meaningful matter slipped by during the 29th of September meeting without any controversy, when members agreed that the Committee's questions to the Minister should be sent to her in advance of her appearance before the Committee on the remaining subject matters (pigs and beef) of the Committee's Inquiry.

It had been difficult getting the Minister in front of the Committee for this one, with her offering dates that didn't suit the Committee and vice versa. A date had finally been agreed and members were content that advance notice of the issues would allow her to provide the fullest response to the Committee, which in turn could then inform, and allow completion of, the Committee's final two reports.

Although this was a very specific circumstance, I thought it set an important precedent. The Clerk and I had been reluctant to do much 'pre-warning' of those coming before the Committee up until now, concerned that to do so might undermine the Committee's oversight role.

But we were equally frustrated when an unsighted Minister or Department official had to say that they would need to consider a particular matter and write to the Committee later about it. This slowed things down terribly, and I welcomed the Committee's agreement to this approach, thinking to myself that we should perhaps be doing it more often.

Chapter 16: October 2000 – And what are we doing today?

The pace of our work seemed to increase as the Committee covered more and more ground, meeting five times in October 2000.

Business included an Inquiry evidence session with the Minister and her most senior officials, and other sessions with industry representatives, while evidence was also taken in relation to the Department's second legislative Bill (the Fisheries (Amendment) Bill).

There were further sessions with the Minister and officials on BSE low incidence status and the draft budget as well as on fisheries issues, which remained fully on the Committee's 'radar'.

Members had talked about conducting a further Inquiry into some of the allegations of pricing 'cartels' that had arisen during the current inquiry. I was pleased when the Clerk advised the Committee that since competition policy was a reserved matter, they may find that their conduct of an Inquiry would be *ultra vires* and that they may not then have the benefit of Assembly privilege, which they could hide behind when making specific allegations.

I was also grateful that the Committee had secured the Specialist Advisor's services, and he briefed the Committee on his thinking around first drafts of their beef and pigs sectoral reports. Members were not slow in demanding more from him, and again I was glad this work wasn't all down to me.

I was finding it hard enough to produce what needed to be produced for a full diary of Committee meetings, particularly without Stephen being there to help, but I had the good fortune that Friday the 13th of October saw a newly seconded civil servant called Rosemary attend her first meeting in what had been Stephen's Executive support role. I had a team again.

At that same meeting, John Dallat, who may or may not have been taking advantage of the fact that the Chairman was not in attendance that day, proposed a motion that all future Committee meetings should be completely open to the public (with one exceptional circumstance).

I think there had been some general discussions around this point among MLAs and officials, and ours was not the only Committee to have been going in and out of private session. This move towards greater transparency was, however, where we as staff thought Committees should be heading. The Committee agreed, voting 6:0 in favour, with one abstention (probably George Savage, who was in the Chair that day, taking the usual Chair's voting line).

That was one of two meetings in October which George Savage chaired in Dr Paisley's absence. As we often did for Dr Paisley, the Clerk suggested that we brief George in the Chairman's office beforehand and certainly, at least for one of the meetings, I know we did just that, as George made it particularly memorable.

At the pre-meeting, Martin went through the printed Chairman's brief with George, line by line, explaining everything that needed to be done, who was coming to give evidence, what needed to be asked, what needed to be completed, and so on.

That all seemed to go fine, with much nodding by George, until we made our way the short distance from the Chairman's office to the Committee room. As we went in the door, and they approached their seats at the Committee table, George turned and said to Martin "Ok, Clerk. And what are we doing today?" There was no element of irony or humour in his question. It seemed he taken nothing in during the preceding half-an-hour.

Despite being clearly taken aback, Martin had to get on with it. I think he mumbled something like: "Why don't I just take us through the Chairman's brief, Deputy Chairman?" And so, with another nod from George, he did just that.

Dr Paisley would quite often have asked "Mister Clerk" to lead members through some agenda items, but George's chairing style was passive almost to the point of nonparticipation, until, that is, a subject allowed him to regale members with one of his anecdotes.

George was fond of an anecdote and quite often he would start one, then interject "…and this is true" (presumably for emphasis) before eventually getting to the point. I do remember on one such occasion idly wondering whether we should consider that everything he said was not true, unless he confirmed that it was.

In one of the October meetings, members also agreed to an invitation to visit the Department's Agricultural colleges, and I think there was a brief outing for a few of the members to Greenmount College on the 25th of October.

Thankfully, that visit was much quieter than the last time we'd 'let them out' (so much so that I can barely remember it, but I'm pretty sure no eggs were harmed during that particular trip). I wondered if the Chairman had learned his lesson from the last visit when he advised the team that that he had other business to attend to that day.

During the October meetings, I also had the pleasure of seeing former bosses, colleagues and acquaintances squirming (or sometimes relaxing) at the far end of the Committee table, when they gave evidence to the Committee as DARD officials. I loved observing the different approaches they took with members.

Some were quite clearly resentful about the new accountability arrangements and of having to be there at all – I'd describe them as old school 'civil servants know best, and elected representatives have no business questioning us' types. It always felt like these officials were holding something back that they felt the Committee shouldn't really be hearing. The Chairman and members felt the same, and didn't take kindly to this approach, and these officials generally got a hard time from the Committee, with a much tighter scrutiny of the detail than might have actually been warranted.

The smarter Departmental 'operators' turned on the charm. They sent short, factual, papers beforehand, gave concise straightforward presentations, and deferentially called members "Mister" or "Chairman". They quite often praised the quality of the questions that were being fired at them, and gave what appeared to be straight, honest answers to those questions. Most importantly, they sounded like they knew their subjects inside out.

For these officials, including a former boss whom I really liked and one official whom I counted as a personal friend, the Chairman and members always had a lot of time. And when these officials brought forward policies or proposals that might have been expected to be criticized, or scrutinized very closely, quite often they were given a 'fair wind' and perhaps even nodded through.

At the time, I remember hoping that I was 'taking notes', in case I one day returned to my parent Department and found myself at the other end of the Committee table. That did happen some years later, and I have to admit that I maybe didn't learn as much from the 'charmers' as I should have!

After a busy month, we finally reached the Assembly's Halloween recess, with no Committee meetings held on the 27th of October or the 3rd of November.

It really is hard to describe the relief that we all felt when the members went home to their families, and we went home to ours.

Each recess was becoming a target to be reached. People working in legislatures the world over will probably know that feeling very well indeed.

Chapter 17: November/December 2000 – Tea, beef and prawns

There wasn't really much in the November and December 2000 business that was worthy of note. That's not to say there wasn't a lot of business conducted. Indeed, there was.

The Committee concluded its work on the Fisheries Bill, and, I was relieved to discover, took the decision to back away from the 'cartel' issue so they would not prejudice an ongoing investigation by the Office of Fair Trading.

I remember thinking that the Assembly's Remembrance service on Friday the 10th of November might have potential to cause discord within the Committee, given that it was scheduled to take place at the same time as our Committee meeting. Poppies and remembrance always seemed to be problematic around that time.

Happily, though, our meeting was simply adjourned (by the Deputy Chairman, the Chairman having been delayed) in order to facilitate those members who wished to attend the Service. There was no fuss made by those members who did not, and we were glad of that.

I'm pretty sure it was at some point between the 17th and 24th of November that I got to see another side of Dr Paisley's life. The Committee held three meetings between those dates and the Chairman had attended none of them. That was most unusual.

More unusual still was that Martin and I were then asked to go and brief the Chairman at his home on Cyprus Avenue, Belfast, a large Manse house on a leafy Belfast Street. I don't recall what exact reasons were given for this request, but the Committee was formulating its second Inquiry report at the time (this one covering the Beef industry sector) and I expect that Dr Paisley wanted to ensure he was content with the direction in which things were heading, having missed so many meetings on the trot.

I remember being completely awed by the security presence at the house as Martin drove us in. Gates, barriers, bollards, bunkers and what appeared to be sophisticated surveillance and communication equipment were in abundance. It seemed to me that there was a battalion of security forces in the grounds, although in reality there were probably just a few moving around very quickly.

Once these forces had established who we were, we were allowed into the house and ushered into a 'proper' living room. I wish I'd paid more attention at the time, but from memory, I think there was a lot of dark and old-style furniture – glass cabinets et al, a bit like my Mum and Dad's sitting room, which we were never allowed to play in – and that there was a lovely wooden table on which we spread our papers.

I remember sitting at the table with Dr Paisley and Ian Junior, with Mrs. Paisley (addressed both as Eileen, and Mummy, by

Dr P) serving us tea and home-made treats (I'm sure they were traybakes).

Mrs. Paisley was a lovely lady, very welcoming, but also with an obvious presence about her, and she reminded me a little of my paternal grandmother ('Nana') with whom you would not mess. The house was buzzing, with other family members flitting around, but not disturbing the Doc.

We conducted our business quickly, and I probably sampled more home-cooked goodies than was entirely appropriate. Then it was time to brave the madness outside again and return to our 'ordinary' offices at Parliament Buildings.

On the way back, I thought that it was credit to Dr Paisley and his wife that they were able to conduct a family life with such high levels of security and disruption surrounding them. I understand that there had been a bomb attack at the house in the early seventies, and his profile made Dr Paisley an obvious target for further attacks. I suppose they were well used to it, by November 2000, but I knew that I wouldn't want to live like that.

As December began, I was amused when the Committee agreed, on the hoof as it were, an additional report recommendation about a ban on imports of foreign beef. The Clerk tactfully pointed out to members that their proposed recommendation was not supported by conclusions reached on the basis of the evidence that they had taken.

Despite Dr Paisley having missed the previous three meetings at which the draft report had been considered, he was back in the Chair and was seemingly unperturbed by this inconvenience. He must have taken the view that it was what members thought and agreed, rather than what the evidence necessarily showed, that mattered most, and he was happy to go ahead with the additional recommendation regardless.

That was members' prerogative, I suppose, and it at least demonstrated that they were prepared, and able, to agree on something, even if it was somewhat dodgy. The Clerk had done his job in pointing out the flaw in the recommendation, and he was careful to ensure that I included this in the minutes of proceedings for the relevant meeting[22].

A good Civil Servant would always (at least at that time) have ensured that a true and accurate record of proceedings was kept, particularly so when this also provided cover for their own backsides. I learned a lot from Martin, who was certainly a good Civil Servant.

Arrangements were made for a press launch for the beef report on the 15th of December, with speaking notes organized (by Martin and me) for both the Chair and Deputy Chair. Other members were expected to 'do their own thing' with their local press, but to base their media engagement on the Committee's press release.

The Department had sent a letter to the Committee about its proposed policy on Transmissible Spongiform Encephalopathies (TSEs). These were also part of my DARD

---

[22] Minutes of Proceeding – 1st December 2000 (Paragraphs 5.6-5.7)

chum's remit. BSE (which was a notable TSE) was still on everyone's minds in relation to the beef sector, and while the letter contained good summary information and was well received by the Committee, members thought it such an important subject that they asked the Clerk to secure expert assistance to aid their understanding of the proposed policy.

Having not been able to visit a second College in the earlier visit, members also agreed a delegation should go to Enniskillen College and a date was agreed (30th January 2001) when that should take place.

Great, I thought. Out and about again!

We started to get close to Christmas, but any hopes of a quiet lead up, or an early start, to the holidays were scuppered with the final Committee meeting of the year being held on the 19th of December. Key amongst the business was the outcome of the EU's December Fisheries Council meeting. Wow! Had it really been a year since the last one?

The two 'Popular Front' Fish Producers' Organisations took it in turns to bash the result of the Fisheries Council meeting (and the local Minister's lack of influence on it) which had included a 10% cut in the Total Allowable Catch (TAC) of Nephrops. I had learned from last year's fisheries discussions that this term meant, essentially, the prawn catch.

Notably, though, Nephrops was a word which seemed to tickle Dr Paisley's fancy. He used to smile broadly as he spoke the word clearly, then he would often repeat the word, almost joyously.

To this day, I can hear Dr Paisley's particular pronunciation in my head: "Knee-Frawwps, [smile] Knee Frawwps" with his signature 'whistle' clearly apparent as the 's' came out between his teeth.

That may be a strange memory to have, but it is a very vivid one, and I also remember using the word in my frequent impersonations of the Chairman among my Committee staff colleagues. I'm doing it now as I type this chapter.

The fishermen were also demanding a 'decommissioning scheme' under which they'd be paid multiple thousands of pounds to decommission their boats. Fortunately for the DARD officials, who appeared immediately after the FPOs had again fired up the Committee, they were able to announce that the Department had a plan to seek EU funding for a £6m decommissioning scheme.

There would be a lot spoken about such a scheme over the coming months and, early on, there was quite often a little 'gallows humour' among the Committee's members about progress on some types of decommissioning being quicker than on others. The arms issue had not gone away, and it remained a 'drag' on political relationships throughout the Assembly and its Committees.

In almost the final business of the year, the Chairman alerted members to a letter from the Minister in which she complained about the practice of notes being passed to the Chair (through the Clerk) from the public gallery. This had certainly occurred during the meeting with the Minister on the 8th of December.

With some advance warning and a little research, I had been able to brief the Clerk well for this item, and he was able to assure members that there was nothing in the Assembly's Standing Orders against such a practice, nor could anything relevant from Westminster practice be found in 'Erskine May'[23].

After discussions, there was unanimous agreement among members that passed notes could help ensure the most topical and relevant matters were being raised, and that since the Chairman would consider points raised in this way and ask questions under his own authority, they saw no reason to amend this practice. You could clearly see Dr Paisley's satisfaction with this outcome, considering it as one point chalked up to him.

I also thought it interesting that the SDLP's PJ Bradley (John Dallat was not present at that meeting) did not on this occasion speak up in support of the Minister's position. Fair play, I thought, PJ is clearly not just a Party 'yes' man.

---

[23] Often referred to as 'the Bible of parliamentary procedure' this describes procedures and conventions in the Houses of Parliament

Chapter 18: And what did Santa bring?

And so it was that we had reached the end of another calendar year. The new Assembly session had been hard work, but the months since the last session had finished had also brought opportunities for me personally.

Even in the very early days of the Assembly, it was abundantly clear that the current crop of Clerks could not be expected to manage their current workloads.

Devolution had taken place with five Clerks (all seconded NI Civil Service Principal Officers, or 'Grade 7s') taking care of ten statutory committees. There were also Clerks in charge of Bills, Business and the Committee on Standards and Privileges, as well as a Clerk of Committees. I was never, frankly, sure of what this Clerk's role entailed, but I concede that there was a need to ensure consistency of standards across all the Committees' Clerking resource.

Some more Clerks had been seconded from the Civil Service – a Clerk to the Assembly Commission, and four new Committee Clerks. But that still wasn't enough, so the Assembly authorities developed a recruitment scheme for new Clerks and Principal Clerks. That scheme was only released when it was certain that the Assembly would return from its first suspension.

This wasn't an internal Assembly promotion board – it was open to the whole Civil Service and to external applicants. Crucially, that meant that I wouldn't be precluded from applying even though my current civil service grade was two grades below Grade 7.

This gave me much to ponder. In my current role, because of Martin's responsibilities being split between two Committees, I was already carrying out many tasks that a Clerk might be expected to do, and I seemed to be doing those just fine. But it was a huge step-up in terms of the level of responsibility. Was I ready? Could I do this?

The biggest consideration for me was the possibility of appointment as a Clerk under similar secondments terms (from the NICS) to my current situation, and whether or not the higher equivalent level of Grade 7 would be honoured on my return to the department after secondment. Many of my Assistant Clerk colleagues were in the same boat, as indeed were others in non-clerking roles within the Assembly.

The NICS initially resisted the prospect of recognizing a promoted Clerk as a Grade 7 on his or her return. I think there was a feeling abroad that we had 'gone over to the other side' given the hard time that officials sometimes got from their respective Committees, and that we should be punished (or certainly not rewarded) for that. The Assembly authorities fought against this position, and recognition was eventually agreed.

Shortly after the summer recess, the NI Civil Service was also running a further promotion board to Deputy Principal (DP), which was the normal level to which I would aspire to progress.

I had decided to go for both jobs. Why would I not?

One difficulty I faced was my proven inability to do a good interview, my last NICS promotion board interview being a good example of having not gone brilliantly.

Part of my problem was that candidates weren't allowed written prompts with them in the interview. I always worked off prompts and, without those, my brain seemed to scramble and lose the detail behind important examples of my work.

Worse still, my attempt in the interview to articulate a valid and relevant point about a remote team becoming too insular, and failing to see the wider picture, became scrambled into what must have sounded very like I was saying that "Teamwork is bad".

I had little doubt that I was capable of the higher-level work, and every one of my line managers agreed, but I simply couldn't 'blow my own trumpet' during interview and would keep saying "we" when the panel were looking for "I" in terms of experience and responsibility.

So, it was with some trepidation that I put myself through two separate interviews around a similar time.

My interview for the Clerk position was held on the 26th of September in the centre of Belfast and I suffered some of the usual problems. I should have been able to cite so many examples of Clerk level tasks that I had already carried out, but, on reflection after the interview, I thought I hadn't really made enough of these. Equally, I hadn't been completely terrible, so I felt there was still an outside chance. My NICS interview for Deputy Principal (I think in late November) was ok, but again wasn't as good as it probably should have been.

All I could do now was await the results.

I got my Clerk interview result letter on the 2nd of November. When I opened it, I was sorely disappointed. While I was considered suitable for appointment as an Assembly Clerk, I wasn't placed high enough on the order of merit to get an immediate appointment but would be held in reserve should further vacancies arise.

Worse still, virtually all of my Assistant Clerk colleagues who had chosen to apply for the Clerk post had received a more positive letter. They were all to be appointed immediately as Clerks! We were a fairly tight and small 'community' and I was, of course, pleased for them, while they were genuinely disappointed for me.

I was gutted and felt I might have to cut my losses now and return to the Department, although I knew that my decision might be affected by the result of the DP competition. I really enjoyed the work, the culture and the people in the Assembly.

It was so different than anywhere I'd previously worked, and I didn't really want to go back.

Around three weeks later, I sought some feedback from the recruitment service about my position on the merit order, asking where they had reached on that merit order when making their initial offers of posts to those who had been successful.

Imagine my surprise and delight when five or so days later I received a second letter from the Assembly, telling me that they now considered me suitable for immediate appointment as Clerk! I knew that I hadn't been ruled out in the first letter, and that if some of the people listed turned down their offers, or future positions arose, then I might have a chance. But I didn't expect anything this quickly.

Perhaps there were more appointments made than we had expected. It is certainly the case that Bound Volume 11 of the Official Report lists 19 new Clerks that were not listed in Bound Volume 10, and I don't recall there ever being any indication that there were quite so many Clerking positions to be filled.

Did I care? Not a jot!

There were also some appointments made to the level of Principal Clerk through the same competition, which had promised a responsibility allowance of 5% above Grade 7 pay scales for those successful at that level. Some Clerks had already been recategorized as Principal Clerks before the competition.

So far as I know there was no formal evaluation of, or a business case for, a role at a higher level than a normal Clerk which justified creation of the grade of Principal Clerk (and the award of their associated responsibility allowance).

Perhaps this was considered to be a 'reward' for the very few who had covered the work of what was now to be done by 31 Clerks and Principal Clerks? That is conjecture on my part, but it did seem that the appointment process may not have been fully transparent.

However, none of us 'newbies' had any real reason to complain. Indeed, I felt that, as new Clerks, it was helpful that we could continue to look up to, and seek advice from, those who were now classified as Principal Clerks.

Lo and behold, on the 18th of December, word also came to me from the NICS that my name was on the list of those considered suitable for appointment to the grade of Deputy Principal. The NICS normal only listed enough people to fill current and anticipated vacancies, so that effectively meant that promotion for me would be imminent.

Wow! An embarrassment of riches! Maybe I was able to do a decent interview after all! Now, effectively, I had a choice of two jobs in my Christmas stocking.

After a little pondering, it was an easy enough decision for me to stay with the Assembly, and I think I may even have confirmed this to the Assembly authorities just before I went off on my Christmas leave.

What a Christmas present that was: I was going to be a Clerk!

And given the work I had done with the Agriculture and Rural Development Committee, and Martin's affinity with, and preference for, the work of his second Committee, I thought it very likely that I would soon be appointed as Dr Paisley's next "Mister Clerk".

How exciting was that? Very exciting indeed, but a little bit terrifying too.

Chapter 19: Paul takes the reins, and the Committee gets some Frank advice

Sure enough, shortly after Christmas, I was told that I was to take over as Clerk to the ARD Committee. Much the same thing occurred across the board, with several other former Assistant Clerks being appointed as Clerks to their 'home' Committees.

I don't think they had been offered any say in the process, but Dr Paisley and George Savage seemed to be quite satisfied with this, particularly in terms of continuity for the Committee. By now, I was confident that they trusted me, and the Chairman was also quite content when I indicated to him my intention to continue Clerking in a manner similar to Martin's.

My appointment hadn't come through by the first meeting back on the 12th of January 2001, however, so our Clerking roles were unchanged for that meeting – I was still in the 'back seat'.

Martin had, as instructed, asked the Assembly's Research Services to secure specialist advice on maters raised just before Christmas, and our researcher, Kevin, proposed an individual called Frank who would provide the Committee with a written report on two subjects: TSEs and the Animal Waste Directive.

After hearing from him (in person) about his understanding of the terms of reference and the short deadlines for the reports, the Committee then formally appointed Frank to do the work. I didn't know it that day, but that appointment would provide my first real test as a Clerk.

At the same meeting, the 'John Dallat versus Dr Paisley' dynamic took another twist, as the former once again raised (under 'Matters Arising' from the last meeting) the issue of notes being passed from the public gallery, thus supporting his Party colleague's (the Minister's) view and going directly against the Chairman's (and indeed the Committee's).

Dr Paisley was inclined to stick to his guns, given the Committee's decision, but, in the interest of fairness, he agreed that the Clerks should seek further advice on the matter. I realized that, from here on in, carrying out that sort of instruction would ultimately be my responsibility, and that was a sobering thought.

I was formally appointed as a Clerk on the 16th of January, and I 'took over' responsibility from the following meeting (which was held on 19th January). Symbolically, my name appears above Martin's in the next two meetings' minutes of proceedings. His attendance at these meetings (sitting close by, but away from the Committee table) was a very helpful way to hand over, and Martin was careful to only offer his help or his view whenever I sought it.

I hope that I articulated to Martin, at the time, my appreciation for his guidance and mentoring throughout the period we worked together. Without his encouragement, and his belief in my abilities, I doubt very much whether I would have applied for, or been able to take on, the Clerk's responsibilities. If I forgot to give my heartfelt thanks to him then, I do so now.

At my first meeting, I was really nervous, but I was doing my best to look relaxed. I clearly remember the great deep breath that I took as I sat at Dr Paisley's side just before he called the meeting to order that day.

I had taken the pre-briefing meeting with the Chairman (also very nervously) and had forewarned him that there would be visitors from Sweden sitting in the gallery. In his opening comments, Dr Paisley pointed this out to the members, directly welcoming the visitors with great gusto and a cheery wave. I knew that it wasn't normally considered to be in order for the Chair to refer to the Gallery. Wisely, however, I let that slight indiscretion go without comment. I was underway.

The meeting wasn't without its hairier moments. Very early on, three of the members expressed concern that a press release that had issued under the Chairman's authority after the last meeting had not conveyed the views of all the members. That raised tensions somewhat, and I wasn't quite sure what to advise, as I understood that Martin had agreed the press release directly with the Chairman.

In a somewhat muted response (which suggested that he knew he was in the wrong) Dr Paisley muttered something about

134

believing it had been an accurate enough summary of views, and (thankfully) the three members left it at that. Post-meeting press releases had been an issue from the Committee's early days, and this 'shot across the bows' from unhappy members suggested to me that I'd need to be very careful over managing the content of the next few that issued.

In my first 'solo run' at taking members through their business (and with an audibly shaky voice) I advised the Committee that I had approached the Clerk Assistant (Murray Barnes, at that point our highest authority on Clerking matters) on the issue of receiving advice from the public gallery during meetings. It seemed that it was an issue that had been raised in Committees other than ours too, and Murray had undertaken to consider the matter further and advise us all. The Chairman and members seemed happy enough to park that for now.

Much of the rest of that first meeting was members' line-by-line consideration of the Pigs sector draft report, which had been mainly put together by the specialist advisor appointed for that purpose, but which I had edited to better fit the committee 'style'. The format for carrying out this task had been well established during consideration of the Committee's first two reports, and I was very comfortable with helping the Committee follow this format again.

There was little argument over the content, and agreement was fairly easily reached on the report's conclusions and recommendations, which, it has to be said, contained a few criticisms of the Department. The lack of acrimony on this subject definitely helped settle my 'first-night' nerves.

The Chairman called an additional meeting on the following Monday (the 22nd of January). It was to be a one issue meeting, about the discovery of spinal cord in beef imported from Germany, and senior officials from DARD and the Food Standards Agency were to brief the Committee on the subject.

Suddenly, it was me that had been approached (by Ian Junior) to arrange the extra meeting and the responsibility was all mine to ensure that members were suitably informed. It was all quite daunting, but Martin agreed to sit in on this additional meeting too, which gave me some welcome support.

It was unusual for the Committee to sit on an Assembly Plenary day, and at one point, George Savage had to leave the Committee's meeting to speak in the Assembly Chamber on the Committee's behalf. The Assembly was debating the Consideration Stage of the Fisheries (Amendment) Bill and George was called to report the outcome of the Committee's deliberations during the Committee Stage.

Obviously, I couldn't be in the Chamber at the same time as Clerking the meeting, but I had prepared a good speaking note for George (another responsibility) and when we checked the Official Report the following day, he seemed to have stayed 'on message' ok.

By that stage we had reached an agreement with Hansard colleagues that we would supply them with a typed (or emailed) copy of such 'set-piece' speaking notes. That way, Hansard would know (and report) what the Member was supposed to be saying in case he or she got a bit mixed up. That would subsequently prove to be a useful convention.

The Committee meeting only lasted an hour and twenty minutes and the members were all 'singing from the same hymn sheet'. Dr Paisley suggested, and members agreed, that a press release should issue, and to avoid any repeat of the previous concerns, I cobbled this together on the spot for members' immediate agreement.

At members' instruction, I also issued a letter to the Minister, in which the Committee encouraged her to take advantage of this situation and lobby for the ban on Northern Ireland beef to be lifted. These action points were very straightforward from a Clerking perspective, which again helped me settle in.

So that was it for the handover. From here on, I'd be flying completely on my own. In cinematic terms, the original 'Mister Clerk' was no longer 'playing' at the Committee theatre.

I was nervous, but also thrilled, that 'Mister Clerk 2, the sequel' was about to be released. Would this be a blockbuster success, or might it be a resounding flop?

Chapter 20: Advisor trouble brews and a horse rides to the rescue

It didn't take long before 'Mister Clerk 2' had his capabilities tested.

At the very next meeting (on the 26th of January) I had the unenviable task of telling members that I didn't believe the recently appointed Specialist Advisor, Frank, had met the Committee's Terms of Reference in a report he had provided on the Animal Waste Directive.

I had double-checked my doubts with our Assembly Researcher, Kevin, and he concurred. Despite Frank's apparent qualifications and experience (which Kevin had relayed to the Committee) Frank's draft report was incomplete. Indeed, it seemed to entirely miss the point of what the Committee had sought.

Members were not amused, and agreed to consider the draft themselves before the next meeting, but, in what I took to be a demonstration of their trust in my (and Kevin's) judgement, they instructed me to take things up urgently with the Advisor, and to stress to him that he must meet the terms of reference.

Furthermore, the Committee's response to the Minister on the subject of the Animal Waste Directive was now due, and the

Chairman therefore instructed me to get the Advisor to appear before the Committee at the next meeting (to be held on the 2nd of February).

Meanwhile, the members went ahead with a visit to Enniskillen College on Wednesday the 31st of January. This was, of course, my first outing as the Clerk, and I definitely felt much more responsibility for how members 'behaved' and for ensuring they didn't get lost.

Once again, Dr Paisley had found something else to do, so was unable to attend, and Gardiner Kane was the only DUP member there. The visit was really interesting and enjoyable and being able to see a galloping racehorse really close up was most exhilarating. The whole trip almost went without incident, too, right up until a local press photographer asked for a photograph of the visiting members and the hosts.

Gardiner approached me and took me off to one side. He appeared quite anxious and distressed, and said that he couldn't appear in a photo alongside the Sinn Fein member (I am sure this was Gerry McHugh, as he was one of the local MLAs). I understood that Gardiner's constituents (and party colleagues) might not be amused to see this, but there were so few members in the Committee delegation that day that he and Gerry both really needed to be included to make the photograph worthwhile.

I had a quiet word with the College Principal (whom I knew from my DARD days) and together we hatched a 'cunning plan'. One of the stable staff was dispatched and quickly

139

returned with one of the biggest horses I had ever seen – well, maybe they're all big when they're that close.

I approached Gardiner and suggested we put him on one side of the horse and Gerry on the other. He thought that might work and sure enough, with the huge horse now in the middle of the frame, there was sufficient distance (and a suitably large barrier) between the two members to make it less uncomfortable for Gardiner, although I think he was very careful not to smile in case it might look like he was enjoying himself.

When I saw the finished photo, I thought that the horse looked very pleased with itself, carrying out important diplomatic duties. I must admit to being pleased with myself too.

Solutions, not problems! Quality Clerking. That's what I'm about now, I thought.

More solutions were soon needed.

When the 2nd of February meeting opened up, the Specialist Advisor found himself being grilled for around forty minutes and the members were very much less than impressed. Once he had left, the Committee was unanimous in their agreement that his work was simply not acceptable.

I was pleased, and pleasantly surprised, when members formally recorded their gratitude for the work that Kevin and I had put in trying to make some sense of Frank's report. Between our work and answers that the members had (painfully) wrung out of Frank, I told members that I thought

I could distill something that could be used as the Committee's response to the Minister, and they then instructed me to do just that.

It was clear that the 'Specialist' advice being given was not of sufficient quality and members were concerned (as was I) at the inefficiency of the Committee and Research teams having to wade through the advice to get anything useful.

Members were also concerned that they were due to respond to the Department very soon on the second issue (TSEs) on the Advisor's terms of reference. Encouraged strongly by Dr Paisley, they therefore instructed me to stop Frank from doing any further work (including on the TSEs issue) and to terminate his contract immediately.

Oh heavens! What did I know about terminating contracts? Trying to clear my head, I quickly agreed to do what I could, but I indicated that I expected that some fees would be due to the Advisor for work already carried out (despite its poor quality).

I told members my understanding was that the contract had been a 'standard' one for all Committees that had been drawn up through consultation between the Assembly's Research Service and the Clerk of Committees. I was instructed by the Committee to seek advice from them both.

When I followed this up, it became clear that the contract wasn't a great help, from the Assembly's point of view, in terms of enforceable clauses relating to the standard of work. But working with those colleagues, and consulting with the

Assembly's legal adviser, Hugh, I issued a letter of termination to Frank early in the following week.

That felt very grown up and responsible, but I was also worried that having my name on the letter meant that any legal challenge to it was also likely to have my name on it.

I was starting to wonder whether the Grade 7 salary (which was, admittedly, a significant step up for me) was worth it.

The next meeting, on the 9th of February, came too early for any resolution of the matter, but members noted, and were content, that the termination letter had issued.

By now, in any event, there were much bigger fish for the Committee to fry. The Chairman indicated that he had been briefed by the Minister about some positive BSE tests on casualty animals, and senior department officials were now present to brief the whole Committee.

Apparently, there had been 54 positive cases out of around 2500 samples taken. This could (with no hyperbole this time) be catastrophic for the beef sector in Northern Ireland in terms of its hopes of getting the BSE export ban lifted.

The officials briefed members in closed session first, fielding several questions. Then the Chairman opened the meeting to the public and the officials read out a prepared statement, and further questions were asked and answered. Much reassurance was given, including the fact that these animals were never destined for the food chain, and that only older animals had tested positive, all the younger animals testing negative.

This 'news management' approach was a new way of doing things, and, even as it was happening, it felt to me like the Committee was being used by the Department.

When I considered this more closely, I could certainly see the attraction for the Department in engineering events this way. The Committee's meeting (which was full of press people) gave the Department a forum through which it was able to get a message of reassurance out to the public (through the media) quickly, while the cross-party nature of the Committee meant that a political consensus could also be quickly established and publicly articulated.

It was also clear that this issue was bigger than petty (or even more serious) party political posturing. If Dr Paisley felt the Committee was being manipulated, he didn't mention it. His interest seemed more to be in the Committee playing its part in supporting the beef industry in what (he saw) was its hour of need.

This was further demonstrated through his insistence on the issue of a Committee press release containing a message of support for the Minister's approach and endorsement of the effectiveness of measures in place in Northern Ireland to protect the consumer.

Once again, I felt that the Assembly structures were offering politicians a way to rise above their usual tribal instincts and my hopes and spirits were raised once more. It also demonstrated that Dr Paisley was capable of operating beyond his usual comfort zone of hyper-critical opposition. I just thought it was a pity that it seemed to take a crisis or sectoral hardship to bring about these improvements, but better that than nothing, I reckoned.

Further business that day saw me set out the arrangements for the forthcoming launch of the pigs sector report. I did a little Clerk ass-covering by issuing members with a list of media contacts that I proposed to invite to the launch. I thought it might be a little thin, but by asking members to come to me if they had any more names to add (knowing full well that no-one would do that) I should be safe from any criticism. I was quickly learning the darker arts of Clerking!

Despite the BSE niceties, there was still a bit of a power struggle going on between the Committee and the Minister. The Minister was resisting Friday appearances, as she hoped to conduct constituency work those days. She offered Wednesday meetings, but there were no Committee rooms available on Wednesdays, and members had other commitments.

At my suggestion, by way of compromise, members agreed that I should convey their request that she set aside one Friday per month, but that the Committee would not insist on that being used unless it was really needed.

I didn't just make that up. I knew the Minister's Private Secretary, Michael, very well. He had been one of my staff in my Rural Development days and had had a 'meteoric' three-grade rise himself from Administrative Officer to Staff Officer in a very short time. He and I had agreed beforehand

144

that this seemed to be a fair compromise and we'd agreed to do our best to sell this to our respective Principals, so I was confident that the Committee's suggestion would be positively met.

The 9th of February meeting also saw members acknowledge that my Executive Support staff member, Rosemary, had been successful in a promotion board, and they wished her every success in her new post. I was delighted for her, too, but it meant that I was now very short of staff. A Committee team generally, by now, had four staff including the Clerk and I was now down to two.

In fairness, the Assembly authorities managed to help me out and by the time of our next meeting (the 23rd of February, having launched the pigs report on Friday the 16th) I had a new Assistant Clerk, Bertie, in place. I also had a new Executive Support officer, John, who had been with the CAL Committee from the outset and was very highly thought of.

I think it appropriate that I say a quick word here about Bertie, because his decision to work with us said a lot about the Assembly's staff in general. Bertie let me know very early on that he was hard of hearing, very significantly so in one ear. He elaborated that his hearing loss was as a result of being caught up in one of the many infamous bombings in Belfast, at the Abercorn bar in 1972. That bombing, which killed two and left more than 130 injured, many horrifically, was widely understood to have been the work of the IRA.

My own exposure to 'the Troubles' was limited to my reasonably close proximity (100 yards) to a car bomb explosion in 1981, when shrapnel fell around me as I took cover behind a low wall. Yet here was Bertie, much more directly affected, volunteering to work with a Committee whose membership included two MLAs from the IRA's 'political wing', Sinn Fein. I accept that nearly 30 years had passed since his traumatic experience, but I thought it an excellent example of the hope that was being invested by so many in the political process.

In any large body of staff, the expectation would be that a fair proportion would have had some connection with 'the troubles', with hurt and harm caused by, and to, all sides. That was, I'm certain, the case with the Assembly secretariat, as we'd come to be known, and our ability to serve all members equally and impartially regardless of these connections was (and remains) a matter of great pride to me.

I endeavoured to get Bertie and John up to speed with our workload quickly. I felt fortunate (and pleased) that they were giving every indication of being quick to learn and very good at their jobs. It turns out that they needed to be.

I had begun to think that the problems and issues that had arisen since I had taken over as Clerk were coming in waves, but little did I know that they were about to turn into a tsunami, and that the Minister was about to become much more acquainted with the Committee than our compromise 'once-a-month' agreement.

Chapter 21: This time it is a crisis

With no meeting held on the 16th of February while the pigs report was launched, the next meeting was held on the 23rd of February, and it had a sombre start. The Minister attended (somewhat ironically, at her request) to brief the Committee on an outbreak of Foot and Mouth Disease (FMD) in England.

The Minister explained that while there was some concern that pigs from Northern Ireland might be involved, there were no clinical signs of the disease on those farms. However, the Minister said that she had put a temporary ban in place on GB imports and had arranged cleansing and disinfecting of vehicles. The EU had put in place a ban on UK goods, including those from Northern Ireland, but the Minister said that she was already pressing for 'regionalisation' for Northern Ireland.

The situation was clearly of concern to members. Remember that many of them were farmers themselves and they would have had personal concerns as well as wider strategic ones. The Minister's response was met with strong support from the Committee, which George Savage was chairing in Dr Paisley's absence. Indeed, the Committee's press release immediately after the meeting commended the Minister and her staff for their actions.

I assumed that the 'greater good' element would again bring unanimity of purpose among the Committee. That was certainly the case at the beginning of the crisis, but I was rather naïve in thinking that it could last forever.

The 23rd of February meeting covered plenty of other business too. I was able to secure members' reluctant agreement to a reduced fee that I had negotiated with the 'Specialist' advisor. It went against the grain for members (and for me too) to pay him anything at all for the work he had produced, but I had to take into account the clear legal advice that I received on the matter, and the members took me at my word.

Over the next couple of weeks, there was a slight wobble when it appeared that the advisor was going back on the negotiated settlement and was insisting on continuing his work, but that turned out to be letters crossing in the post, and Frank eventually signaled acceptance of our terms, accepted payment and 'went away'. Although I knew that members weren't completely satisfied at the money wasted, I was happy to have achieved a result that avoided what could have been a protracted legal battle.

Now that both the beef and pigs reports were published, Members agreed that the Committee should seek an Assembly debate on the two reports around the 26th of March. They also now wanted to start up new Inquiries and subjects were mooted including the Livestock and Meat Commission (LMC), the Department's disaster planning and, following a critical report from the Public Accounts Committee (PAC), DARD's Rural Development Programme.

Thinking of the workload potential, I urged members to consider subjects that would lend themselves to short, focused Inquiries in the future, bearing in mind how long it had been since the first one had begun. In turn, Members instructed me to develop terms of reference (ToRs) for several inquiries that they could consider. I could, at least, control what I put in front of them.

I also had some concerns about my potential role in marshalling evidence the Committee might hear about any of the department's work areas in which I had been personally involved, such as Rural Development. I decided to keep my concerns to myself and wait to see what the Committee decided. I reckoned that the Rural Development ToRs could virtually write themselves given the specific nature of the PAC Report's criticisms, so I thought that the danger of a conflict of interest at this stage was low. I was, however, aware of it.

Finally, on the 23rd of February, I had an inward chuckle when George Savage suggested, from the Chair, that because Northern Ireland was a region of a Member State of the EU, it would be a good thing for the Committee's knowledge of Europe to be expanded, perhaps by a visit to Europe.

It was a widely held view that Northern Ireland politicians (particularly Councillors) were often keen on taking up opportunities to 'broaden their experience' on expenses, and I considered George's comments to be blatant angling for a Committee 'junket'. I wasn't sure how to respond. However, other members, to their credit, wisely suggest that there needed to be a specific, suitable and relevant issue to justify the Committee's involvement in such a trip, with its associated costs to the public purse.

I agreed completely with that line, although the thought of having to look after members on a foreign visit filled me with dread.

The following week's meeting, on the 2nd of March, gave a clear indication of where the Committee's focus would lie over the next period.

The Fish Producers Organisations were first into the room, and their demeanor suggested that their position had clearly worsened since their last visit. Both delegations were robust in their criticism of the lack of action from DARD on several issues.

But they may as well not have been there, for all the attention members were paying to their plight that morning. They were very much the 'undercard' for the main event, which was a further update on the Foot and Mouth situation. It had now got considerably worse, with an outbreak of the disease having occurred in South Armagh.

Indeed, DARD's Fisheries officials had to wait until the FMD 'show' was over before they got to respond to the FPOs' criticisms. Their performance wasn't very convincing, and I recognized some clear stalling tactics on their behalf (having used similar ones myself in the past), but the Committee didn't really pick them up on this as their collective minds were elsewhere.

150

For the FMD session, the Minister had come to the Committee table, flanked by the Permanent Secretary, Peter Small, and the Chief Veterinary Officer, Bob McCracken. Both officials were well known to the Committee and, crucially, both had the confidence of members. Bob, in particular, had an obvious command and knowledge of the subject, and a way of simplifying explanations so they could be easily understood. In short, the delegation had credibility.

The Chairman had told me to arrange for the session to be recorded and transcribed by the Hansard people, which was not the usual form for Committee meetings at the time. While I knew this would cause some difficulties for the Editor of Debates in terms of staffing, he agreed that it was a reasonable request given the seriousness of the subject[24].

The Minister's statement outlined policies of exclusion zones and the slaughter of animals, together with closure of the Department's colleges and forest parks. It was becoming clear that this crisis was going to affect the wider public as well as the farming community, and the mood in the room was deadly serious.

Dr Paisley chaired the meeting very skilfully, and with the gravity that was appropriate, and members took their lead

---

[24] I could find no 'Minutes of Evidence' for the Committee dated the 2nd of March 2001 archived on the Assembly website, but there are references, in the archived minutes of evidence for the 9th of March, to there having been a 'Hansard' for the earlier meeting, although the Chairman added that it had been "recorded unofficially".

from him, resulting in exchanges that were business-like and non-confrontational.

The Minister called for full co-operation from everyone during the crisis. While this was ostensibly aimed at farmers and the public, there was a clear message there too for the Chairman and members of the Committee. For their part, the members again expressed their appreciation for the Minister's work and that of her officials.

Would this cordiality continue? The Minister had mentioned that there appeared to have been smuggling of sheep involved in the local outbreak.

Unfortunately, the words "smuggling" and "South Armagh" were synonymous at the time, and I expected that, given the demographic in that area, it may not be long before political capital could be sought by elements within the Committee.

I wasn't wrong.

Chapter 22: The Gloves come off

Given the wider public interest in FMD, the Minister made a statement to the Assembly at its plenary meeting three days later, on the 5th of March[25]. We were, by now, able to catch plenary business on the Assembly's internal TV system and I remember trying to listen to it as I carried out the usual post- and pre-meeting tasks that day. I was really only interested, though, in Committee members' contributions.

The Minister reported some further information on the wider response to the outbreak, which now included the banning of livestock auctions and markets, advice to the public not to visit the countryside, and a request for sporting event organisers to consider whether their events were necessary. My goodness, I thought. Sport being affected. This was getting really serious.

Dr Paisley, as Chairman of the ARD Committee, was (in accordance with usual practice) called to ask the first question to the Minister following her plenary statement. After (true to form) using the words "catastrophe and a crisis" in his first sentence, he immediately went on the attack, referring to the Minister's "friends in the South of Ireland" who, he said, over

---

[25] Official Report Bound Volume 9 pages 349-360

the weekend had suggested that the RoI response had been better than Northern Ireland's.

I stopped what I was doing, to listen more closely. I felt very uneasy about what he was saying, since it was arguable that, in being called as Chairman, he should have been articulating the Committee's views, unless he made it clear that he was articulating his own, which he had not.

Ian Junior weighed in shortly afterwards with an almost inevitable question asking the Minister to substantiate claims that Republicans were behind much of the smuggling trade in the area, while another party colleague asked if she wanted the (British) security forces patrolling the NI side of the border, as the Irish forces were doing on their side.

Dr Paisley's change of tack from three days earlier was disappointing to me, but not particularly surprising, since the bigger picture context at the time was one of low levels of political trust.

The IRA was only just resuming contact with the Decommissioning body, but no arms were yet 'beyond use', and an Assembly debate (on the 27th of February) on security force collusion had been particularly rancorous. So, I reckoned that some sniping could be expected in the Chamber, and members didn't disappoint.

This behavior didn't (to my relief) immediately translate fully to the Committee, however. Whether or not that had to do with the proximity of their political opponents across the table, or the fewer numbers of party colleagues available with which to gang up, I don't know, but the Committee meeting on the 9th of March[26] (with the Minister again in attendance) started off with the Chairman and members in reasonable form.

Indeed, the Chairman opened with an apology to the Minister for not sending her a copy of the Hansard of the previous week's meeting (which had ultimately been my responsibility, so that was a bit awkward for me).

The Chair also sought to be scrupulously fair to members who'd missed out on asking questions the previous week, ensuring they got to ask their questions first.

There were a few little digs from the 'usual suspects': Ian junior asking the Minister if she had made personal contact with the RUC Chief Constable, John Dallat having a go at others for making political capital, and Francie Molloy welcoming the restrictions on meat and animals from England, Scotland and Wales.

However, the session was reasonably friendly and ended on a very positive note, with the Chairman asking the Minister to convey, to her officials, members' appreciation of the strain that the officials were working under. For her part, the Minister thanked the Committee for members' concern, interest and co-operation.

---

[26] See archived minutes of evidence for the Committee for Agriculture and Rural Development for that date on the NI Assembly website

I found the comparison between what was going on in plenary and in Committee really interesting. It was almost like there were two Dr Paisleys in play – the Committee one acutely aware of and constrained by the responsibilities of his office, the other seemingly free of those shackles.

After the Minister left that meeting, members agreed my draft terms of reference for a further two Inquiries: the first on the LMC (adding one subject matter to the limited number suggested by me) and on the Rural Development Programme (unchanged to those I'd drafted). Members were of the view that their normal business should proceed, regardless of the current crisis.

The Minister's next FMD statement in the Assembly Chamber, on Monday the 12th of March,[27] saw a significant spat between two of our Committee members.

The Minister and the Department had been adamant that all events should be carefully considered by their organisers, with the advice that any that would involve large numbers, and/or movements involving rural communities, should really not go ahead. In her statement, she thanked the authorities from GAA, rugby and soccer who had all cancelled events.

Gerry McHugh did not waste the opportunity this presented, as he gleefully asked the Minister about the proposed General Assembly of Dr Paisley's Free Presbyterian Church, which was scheduled to take place the following week in Belfast's

[27] Official Report Bound Volume 10 pages 1-10

Odyssey Arena, and what her view was on whether it should be cancelled.

Ian junior was absolutely livid at this clear attack on his Dad, and hissed "Papish Bigot", a comment which was then referred to by another member, querying whether it constituted 'unparliamentary language' (which could result in a member's expulsion from the Chamber) and thus ensuring the comment would appear in the Official Report. Presumably in the interests of fairness and consistency, Ian Junior called the other MLA a papish bigot too!

The Deputy Speaker who was chairing the Plenary session said he would refer the matter to the Speaker, who subsequently (on the 20th of March) ruled that the insult was unparliamentary, but that the member using it couldn't have known that at the time, as it had not been the subject of a previous ruling.

The Speaker, citing "natural justice", took no retrospective action against Ian Junior, but I feared that the scene was now set for fireworks in the smaller Committee setting.

The Committee's next meeting was held on Friday the 16th of March, and, in a way, I wasn't unhappy when Ian Junior made me aware that Dr Paisley was to be recorded as an 'apology' for the meeting, as I believed that members seemed much less ready to 'kick off' when George was in the Chair.

Whether or not that had a bearing, or if wiser heads had 'had a word' I don't know, but while the two members concerned were by no means exchanging pleasantries, there wasn't too much overt antagonism evident either.

The Minister briefed the Committee[28] that things appeared to be looking up in relation to FMD. There was still only one confirmed case in Northern Ireland (while GB was being ravaged by multiple outbreaks) and there was talk of relaxation of movement controls. There were even thoughts of relaxing some of the wider controls, with the Easter tourist season almost upon us.

The Minister also pre-empted some potential point-scoring by saying that there was joined-up government across the Assembly's Executive in response to the crisis, and that the Army and the RUC were part of that joined-up approach.

In turn, and somewhat surprisingly, Ian Junior's and Gerry McHugh's questions did not appear to be aimed at scoring points either. The DUP's Gardiner Kane even went as far as commending the Minister and her Department, while the UUP's Billy Armstrong said that NI was fortunate to have its own Government at Stormont. Even Boyd Douglas, the independent Unionist, congratulated the Minister.

Was the Committee back on an even keel, all working for the greater good? Not completely, since members then managed to fall out over the scheduled Speaker's St Patrick's day reception at Parliament Buildings, to which 150 people had

---

[28] See archived minutes of evidence (relating to FMD) for the Committee for the 16th of March

been invited. This was well known as an exclusive and enjoyable event, and invitations to it were highly prized.

The Speaker had sent a letter to the Committee during our meeting asking for its views on whether the event should be cancelled or proceed. The letter was delivered by the Speaker's office (I assume deliberately) just after the Minister had left, and I was asked to read it aloud to members.

I personally thought it quite unfair for the Speaker to put the onus for this decision on the Committee, particularly at such short notice. I could see the attraction for the Speaker in being able to point to the Committee's view when defending either the event's cancellation, or its going ahead, but I thought it a bit of an 'ambush', as did some of the members.

John Dallat quickly jumped in to propose that the Committee tell the Speaker not to proceed with the event. Billy Armstrong attempted to secure support for a compromise (or buck-passing, depending on your view) amendment, to instead ask the Speaker to take the views of the Minister and the Chief Veterinary Officer before deciding.

The amendment went to a vote (my first as Clerk), falling as a result of a 3:3 tie, and the original motion then also fell with a 3:4 vote against. The Committee agreed that I should pass on those results to the Speaker's office. This meant that the Speaker didn't get the 'cover' he had hoped for, but, from memory, he cancelled the event in any case.

As the meeting was about to finish, Ian junior returned to a question he had put to the Minister as to whether she thought it would be useful for the Committee to conduct an investigation into the outbreak to "help" the Department. Ian put the subject forward as yet another possible subject for a further inquiry. I sensed that this wasn't altogether an altruistic suggestion, and that it might be more indicative of an appetite to find fault.

I suspected that he and others in his party might be perturbed, perhaps even disappointed, by the apparent widespread recognition that the Minister (and the department) had responded well to the crisis. Certainly, the Minister's grasp of the topic and ability to field questions on it had grown before our eyes, both in the Committee and plenary sessions.

Before other members could comment on Junior's suggestion, I reminded the Committee that it had already taken a decision on this matter, two weeks previously. Their earlier decision was that it would not be appropriate to conduct such an inquiry while the situation was ongoing. My intervention seemed to put that idea to bed, for now, but I wasn't sure that Ian Junior would let it go that easily.

Finally, a motion was agreed for tabling, seeking a debate on the 26th or 27th of March, and asking for the assembly's endorsement of the Committee's two reports on the beef and pigs sectors. I went straight from the Committee room to the Business Office and tabled the motion.

Tensions mounted again during the Committee's next meeting (on the 23rd of March) after the Minister reported an outbreak of FMD just across the border in County Louth from where the NI outbreak had occurred.

This time Dr Paisley and Ian Junior 'ganged up' on the Minister to criticize what they perceived as a danger to achieving regionalization for NI in her 'tying herself' to the South, when she did not previously tie herself to Great Britain's approach. Not surprisingly, Gerry McHugh weighed in with a criticism of being tied with GB which, he said, was the source of the problem.

Not to be left behind on the point-scoring front, John Dallat asked the Minister for her views on the message being sent out by MLAs given that one Committee member was planning to go to Scotland, when such travel was being discouraged. After much consternation and raised voices, it ensued that Gardiner Kane was the member in question, and Dr Paisley complained that this was "very cheap politics" on John Dallat's part. "Pot, kettle and black", I'll admit to thinking to myself, given his own tactics at times!

Of his 'Jekyll and Hyde' personalities, the 'responsible Chairman' Dr Paisley seemed to be taking a back seat that day, with his more strident (and truculent) character in the lead. In my view, letting that happen was a mistake on his part, and meant that, in my perceived contest between the Minister's and the Chairman's respective performances during the crisis, Dr Paisley was definitely coming second.

A further point went to the Minister during questions following her Plenary statement on the 26th of March, when

Dr Paisley complained about the relative speed with which the RoI had achieved regionalization while NI still had not. The Minister fired back that the difficulty arose since NI had to make its case to the EU through the UK (as a region of a Member State) while the South could make its own case. He had no answer to that!

In other business, the Assembly debated the motion seeking endorsement of the Committee's Beef and Pigs reports on Tuesday the 27th of March[29]. I had provided decent speaking notes for both the Chairman and Deputy Chairman, to ensure they covered as much ground as possible between them.

There was a little flurry of activity during the debate when Dr Paisley said that the Committee hadn't yet received the Minister's response to one of the reports, and there seemed to be a suggestion from the Minister's benches that one had been sent. I was able to get a note to the Chairman that we definitely hadn't received the reply and he referred, in his speech, to having consulted me about it.

I remember that I was uncomfortable being directly mentioned on the floor of the Chamber, since Clerks were supposed to operate entirely behind the scenes.

On this occasion, I think I had a quick word with the Minister's PS as the Assembly sitting was suspended for lunch, and we sorted the matter out between us, and there was no further mention of it in the Chamber that afternoon.

---

[29] Official Report Bound Volume 10 pages 145-159

After lunch, the point-scoring began again, with Ian Junior taking an intervention from his Dad in which they complained that the Minister wasn't present to hear the debate. Indeed, the numbers in the Chamber were very low for the debate, which disappointed the Chair and some members, but I was quite happy since it meant that the debate might not go on for its full allotted time. In all, nine of the eleven members spoke in support of the motion (I don't think David Ford or Francie Molloy were there) along with two MLAs not on the Committee.

The Minister (now in her place) alluded to the Chairman's lack of understanding about why she was unable to attend for part of the debate. She then welcomed the Committee's reports but gave reasons why some of the 24 recommendations couldn't be met. Dr Paisley said he was disappointed with this, but I didn't think he did it with any great conviction.

Something else had, however, clearly bothered him. As he summed up the debate, he was at pains to point out that the reports represented a collective Committee effort. He was, he said, "sick, sore and tired" of people saying that Committee matters were "Paisley's doing".

It was true that the media often referred to 'Paisley's Committee'. Indeed, my own friends and family frequently teased me that I worked for Paisley. But I didn't (and still don't) know what provoked this particular outburst, although it occurred to me that he didn't help himself when he used his

Committee position to make personal or party-based attacks on opponents.

Dr Paisley went on to argue that none of his political opponents could ever say that he had given them a raw deal from the Chair. I had to laugh when he said (of his pen-pointing tactic): "They all admit that I call them carefully. I call some of them prayerfully, but I do call them all". That might explain his eyes being closed when he taps the table and points his pen, I thought.

A few days later, the Minister's weekly update at the 30[30] of March Committee meeting[30] included some self-congratulation on her part about the achievement of regionalization status for Northern Ireland, particularly in light of the 700 or so cases of FMD that were now in Great Britain. There was still only one outbreak in Northern Ireland, and the Executive had also relaxed some of the restrictions on the general public's movements.

Dr Paisley must have had enough of this unexpectedly good performance from an opponent and the plaudits that were continually coming her way. He had, it seemed, given a radio interview that morning (as Committee Chair) which had seriously ruffled some Committee feathers. Mr. Hyde was in charge once again, it seemed.

I hadn't heard the interview but got a sense of it in the Committee meeting when Dr Paisley went straight onto the

---

[30] See archived minutes of Evidence (FMD) for the 30th of March

attack, accusing the Minister of not being open about negotiations that had taken place with South Armagh farmers who, he alleged, had demanded an amnesty over possible prosecution over smuggling offences (presumably in return for their co-operation with the Department).

He appeared to be quite certain of his ground, no doubt (I thought) having been informed by someone present at the alleged negotiations. It was widely understood that Dr Paisley had a wide network of informants: many 'little birds' out there telling him about many things. And, of course, he rarely lacked confidence in any position that he took.

However, Dr Paisley's behaviour that morning created the biggest sense of hostility I had ever felt within the Committee and, as an inexperienced Clerk, I found that very stressful to deal with.

In the biggest show of Committee disunity yet, three members insisted that I put on record the fact that they distanced, or disassociated, themselves from the Chairman's remarks, while Francie Molloy added his view that the Minister's co-operation with the South had been beneficial in achieving regionalization.

The atmosphere was awful, and all I could do was ensure things were recorded faithfully in the minutes.

For her part, the Minister dealt with the situation calmly, suggesting that his interview perhaps demonstrated that the Chairman didn't quite understand what was going on. That was a clever response, which must have infuriated Dr Paisley, but he didn't really have anything with which to come back to her, and it was through a particularly gritted set of teeth that Dr Paisley thanked the Minister for attending that morning.

During later discussions, Francie Molloy made some reference to apparent internal wrangling among the membership of one of the two farmers' representative organisations, the Northern Ireland Agricultural Producers Association (NIAPA). According to Francie, a certain Sean Clarke was now the spokesperson for farmers in South Armagh and indeed Chairperson of NIAPA in that region.

My ears pricked up at this, since the Committee had asked NIAPA to give evidence for the Inquiry into the LMC. I hoped this internal wrangling situation wouldn't affect the Committee's ability to learn what it needed to learn, but I was concerned that it might.

The Rodgers/Paisley rancour continued into the Assembly Chamber following the Minister's next Plenary Statement (on the 2nd of April), with Dr Paisley again attempting to make mileage of the question of an amnesty being discussed and another Committee member (this time David Ford) distancing himself from the Chairman's remarks.

Later that day, during other agriculture-related business in the Chamber, Dr Paisley went on what I can only describe as a rant, viciously attacking the SDLP's Eddie McGrady for no obvious reason. During this rant he rejoiced at his position as Chairman of the Committee which, he said, because of the rules that people had voted for, was unassailable. Basically: "I'm here, and you can never get rid of me!"

I was beginning to think that these weren't really the actions and words of a completely rational person. Nor did they reflect my experience of the personality of the Chairman with whom I still met regularly.

I wondered whether, at 75, this might all be getting too much for him. These exchanges were also quite clearly damaging the good will and collective approach in the Committee, which he had so carefully fostered at the beginning.

Thankfully, the Easter recess was coming up, and I was also delighted when, for the last meeting before recess on the 6th of April, the Minister didn't appear before the Committee, but sent a written update instead. This allowed the Committee (and Dr Paisley) to calm down somewhat, and to turn to other important business.

The FMD outbreak hadn't slowed down the Committee's other business at all. That day saw two evidence sessions for the LMC Inquiry, one further session with DARD Fisheries officials, discussion of the written FMD update, five 'matters arising' addressed, one Statutory rule considered, a response agreed to the Department on the Rural Development Strategy (on the strength of a Research paper and an evidence session involving my former department boss the previous week), discussion on a pigs grant scheme and nine items of 'other business'.

That was a lot of work. By now, though, I had decided that it would be much more efficient to give the Department's officials some advanced warning about what the Committee might ask them. I mostly did this by briefing the Department's Assembly Liaison Officer (DALO) over the phone. I knew that the ice on which I was skating was quite thin, as it could easily be seen as divided loyalties on my part, but my motivation was to reduce the numbers of meetings and evidence sessions it would take for the Committee to obtain the information it needed.

While I didn't clear my approach directly with Dr Paisley, I set a personal benchmark that I would not divulge anything to DARD that I would not be able to justify to the Chairman, and I often rehearsed what I would say to him if challenged.

Overall, I would say that my strategy worked well, and officials were suitably prepared to cover the points that were most relevant and important to the Committee.

Only once did it nearly unravel, when shortness of time meant that I simply copied my questions (for members) to the Department. The attending official kept saying how good each member's question was, then answering them so comprehensively that it was obvious (to me at least) that he had seen them in advance. Fortunately, the official in question was well known as a 'character' and members just assumed he was being his usual unconventional self.

I got away with that one and, thankfully, never needed to explain myself to Dr P.

Aside from the point-scoring among the few, the rest of the members had, I thought, started to perform their roles pretty well, and they certainly came to life with the LMC Inquiry and the FMD 'sessions'. I suppose the subjects were close to home to the farmer-members, and I thought there was now a fair bit of decent probing and 'holding to account' of the department going on, with subjects such as animal movement restrictions, and livestock mart re-opening being well-aired in public.

In my attempt to get ahead of a potential problem, I alerted the Committee to the fact that, further to what Francie Molloy had previously said, I'd established that there were now two groups that claimed to represent NIAPA and that both wanted to make representations to the LMC Inquiry. At my suggestion, the members agreed that they would listen to all that wanted to give evidence but that the Committee would not get involved in any internal disputes.

That was the plan. Things wouldn't quite work out like that, though.

The day's business at the meeting on the 6th of April was fairly typical, and we really were working flat out as a Committee team. I was absolutely delighted, therefore, when the Chairman brought the meeting to a close and, after a few bits of tidying up, the team and I could start to enjoy our Easter break.

We were only due to have Easter Monday and Tuesday off, but I was going to take some annual leave days off to spend with my wife and young family, to just relax.

Bliss. Or perhaps not.

Chapter 23: Saying it with flowers and an Easter ruined

The start of the Easter holiday didn't go quite so well for my colleagues who worked in the Business and Speaker's Offices.

A massive row broke out, late on Friday the 6th of April and over the weekend, about a display of Easter lilies in Parliament Buildings. Lilies were seen by some as a symbol of remembrance for IRA terrorists and, to others of course, as respectfully representing men and women who died for Irish freedom.

It seems that the Assembly Commission, which is the Corporate Body for the Assembly, had agreed a delicate compromise for a bowl of lilies to be displayed in the Great Hall for two days. In true Northern Ireland fashion, that deal went 'pear-shaped' and, in a move orchestrated by the DUP, sufficient numbers (thirty) of unionist MLAs signed a motion that the Assembly be recalled to discuss this "matter of urgent public importance".

The motion for discussion sought to rescind the Commission's decision. A separate thirty members signed a 'Petition of Concern' about the motion, meaning that it couldn't be passed without cross-community support and was therefore destined to fall.

I remember there being a lot of coverage of this story on the local news, with the usual sides being taken by many, but with fair numbers of the public also articulating their despair at the expense and disruption of an additional Assembly sitting for what didn't sccm to be a life-or-death issue.

It seems that the Speaker didn't allow his Easter plans to be disrupted, as Deputy Speaker Jane Morrice was in the Speaker's Chair on Tuesday the 10th of April for what was a horribly acrimonious debate[31] which ended, inevitably, with the motion falling.

In the debate, some members expressed a lack of surprise that the issue had arisen, or that sectarian tensions were being stoked, relatively close to the Westminster and local government elections, which were scheduled for the 7th of June that year.

I 'couldn't possibly comment' on that, but, whatever the reasons behind the rancour, I thought it likely that relations within the Committee would be pretty frosty when we resumed on the 27th of April as was planned.

I got to find out a little sooner than that.

I remember sitting in my conservatory in our house in Bangor, enjoying some Spring sunshine, when my mobile rang (for I,

---

[31] Official Report Bound Volume 10 pages 277-294

along with the other new Clerks, was now important enough to have been provided with a little Nokia by the Assembly). I think this was on Easter Sunday, as I was really taken aback when I heard Ian junior's voice on the other end, it being the Sabbath and all that.

Junior got straight to the point: "My Dad wants to call an urgent Committee meeting. There's been more outbreaks of Foot and Mouth." He went on to say that I needed to get all the members together for this meeting, and to ensure that the Minister came 'up the Hill' to brief the Committee. I was told I needed to make it happen in the next couple of days.

Apparently an initially negative test for FMD on an animal in Ardboe, County Tyrone had turned out to be positive, with word on that positive result (the second case in Northern Ireland) coming in on Good Friday evening, followed by a third case in Cushendall (confirmed on Saturday). It's hard, in these days of 24 hour 'breaking news' and the immediacy of social media, to imagine that I had not heard any of this by Sunday lunchtime, but all of it was news to me.

Ian junior was most animated during the call, and I thought I sensed in his voice a relish, almost, at the chance to finally have the Minister on the 'back foot' before the Committee, and also for the Chairman to look good at having responded so swiftly to the situation by recalling the Committee.

This was completely unchartered territory for me. I had worked long hours into the evenings with this job, but never on the weekend, and on a holiday weekend to boot! It was a

173

fairly crushing blow, not least because I knew I'd have to ruin my staff's holidays as well as missing out on much-needed relaxation time.

This was also, I realised, another early test of my credentials as 'Mister Clerk' and I was determined not to be found wanting. I told Ian Junior to leave it with me, and that I'd get it done.

Straight away I rang Michael, the Minister's PS, just as he was about to ring me, and he told me that the Minister had acknowledged that she'd need to brief the Committee. Realizing that the extra meeting would have an effect on other Assembly and department staff, such as Doorkeepers, DARD officials and Hansard reporters, Michael and I agreed a plan to avoid the two public holidays on Easter Monday and Tuesday, with Michael suggesting that the Minister would make herself available on the Wednesday (the 18th). I got back to Ian Junior quickly and he agreed those arrangements on his Dad's behalf.

Much of the rest of the day, and Easter Monday, was spent making calls to staff and Committee members. I'm pretty sure I had the Chairman's and all the other members' numbers, in a list on my Assembly phone, as I remember being heart-scared of losing it and some outsider using it to get to any of the members.

In any event, we got to the Wednesday. I recall being unconvinced at the time of the merits of the meeting (which lasted less than an hour-and-a-half)[32] versus the disruption it caused, but I suppose it allowed both the Committee and the Department to be seen to be doing something. It also provided the opportunity for the press to cover matters and give publicity to the Department's messages more immediately than if they had waited until the Assembly was sitting. Apart from Gerry McHugh, there was a full turnout of members ready to hear the grim news.

The Minister set out the current position. Given the location of the further outbreaks, the assumption was being made that it came down to some farmers moving animals (sheep) when they shouldn't have done so. The Minister then reported that regionalization for Northern Ireland had been lost, and that several new measures were being planned as contingencies: culling of animals, potential vaccinations, mobilization of private veterinarians and provision of a new helpline. People, she said, should be prepared for further outbreaks, and the previously deployed 'fortress farming' slogan was wheeled out once more.

Expecting fireworks, and some "you're not so clever now" grandstanding, I was more than surprised at the Chairman's conciliatory tone with the Minister that day, other than pushing her for action on the illegal movement of sheep. Dr Jekyll to the fore, it seemed.

---

[32] See archived Committee Minutes of Evidence (FMD) for the 18th of April

Ian junior had a small 'swipe' at the Minister when comparing the action being taken at Northern Ireland's ports to what was (or wasn't) happening on the border with the Republic, but his heart didn't really seem to be in it, or perhaps he'd been warned off by his dad.

The Minister praised event organisers who had taken the decision to cancel events without being required to. These included an Apprentice Boys parade and a Republican demonstration, GAA and rugby fixtures, a cycle race and the North West 200, an iconic motor-cycle road race on the North Coast which was a vital earner for many of the region's businesses and accommodation providers.

In setting out all of these events, the Minister was, I think, careful to make it clear that all sides of the community were being equally affected. The citizens of Northern Ireland tend to have a default position of checking out the fairness of any situation in terms of 'us' against 'them-uns'.

It seems we can accept hardship, including the temporary loss of cultural expression, if our ones know that those hardships and losses are being felt by them-uns too.

It certainly seemed to work with the Committee, and everyone else appeared supportive of the Department's (and the Minister's) response. Had we again reached a point where a crisis meant that unity was more important than division? Probably not, with elections so close, I thought.

With the next meeting due to be held the following week, I convinced the Chairman that there would be no merit in the

Committee meeting between now and then (even if further outbreaks occurred as expected).

With no other 'special meetings' planned, I returned home and vowed to do my best to forget all about the Assembly (and Foot and Mouth Disease) for a few days, to try to 'recharge my batteries' and to spend some precious time with my family.

Chapter 24: Four updates, one walk out and a Funeral

There was little of note in the Minister's next FMD update to the Committee at the meeting held on the 27th of April[33]. What was more interesting was that members got five subjects for the price of one from her that day, with the Minister spending around two hours fielding questions.

As time went by, there was a developing sense of 'déjà vu', both with the Minister's weekly updates and with members' questions. When she appeared again before the Committee on the 4th of May, reporting no further outbreaks or suspects, the Deputy Chairman and members were happy to agree with the Minister's suggestion that she update the Committee and the Assembly on alternate weeks.

As in many of these situations, the Minister's PS and I had discussed this in advance, and I had also cleared the line with Dr Paisley, even though he wasn't attending that day. So, there were no surprises about this move.

---

[33] Minutes of Evidence (FMD) for the 27th of April do not appear to be archived but the minutes of Proceedings confirm the meeting took place

What was more interesting was the Minister's reference to NIAPA, in response to what I was sure was a planted question from John Dallat.

She told the Committee that she was not going to receive any more delegations from NIAPA until the internal dispute over the organisation's chairmanship had been resolved. This was potentially significant for us, since representatives from what was calling itself the 'NIAPA Ruling Council' were already in the Committee room's public gallery, ready to come to the table and give evidence to the Committee's Inquiry into the LMC. I needed to watch this one, I thought.

The Meat Exporters gave their evidence to the Inquiry first, and from checking the minutes of proceedings that day, I can see that there were eight Committee members attending when the Exporters came in. By the time they left, an hour or so later, both SDLP members had left the meeting, around 20 minutes apart. Billy Armstrong then left before the 'NIAPA Ruling Council' came to the table.

That meant we were down to five members, which was the Committee's quorum. I was on edge by this stage, as I was required by Standing Orders to bring the Chairman's attention to a loss of quorum should that occur.

The three-man delegation, including Sean Clarke, came to the table and George read out a statement I had prepared for him highlighting the Inquiry's terms of reference and restating th Committee's decision about not getting involved in any dispute.

Before the delegation were able to open their mouths, however, the Committee absolutely became involved in the dispute, as Boyd Douglas, Gardiner Kane and Ian Junior pushed back their seats, lifted their papers and left the meeting.

This left George Savage and Gerry McHugh as the only members attending, and the Committee well short of its quorum. With no expectation that any of the members were about to return, George had no option but to bring the meeting to a close there and then. I was not fully up to speed on what was going on within NIAPA, but the moment was pretty embarrassing for George, and for me.

I suppose the fact that Francie Molloy had previously spoken up for Sean Clarke might have been enough to suggest to me that certain other members might not be so supportive of his claim to the NIAPA office. But I was a bit pissed off that the Committee had done exactly what it had agreed not to do. All I could do was to explain the quorum rule to the delegation and apologise for their having wasted their journey that morning.

This issue spilled into the next two Committee meetings as well. On the 11th of May, Francie Molloy proposed a motion to invite the delegation back to hear their evidence. Gardiner Kane countered with an amendment to the effect that the Committee would follow the Minister's example and not receive any NIAPA delegation until the dispute was resolved.

While I obviously wasn't in a position to support either proposal, I thought Gardiner's suggestion was the logical thing to do, since it was consistent with the Department's. A vote was taken on the amendment, and it was quickly apparent that it was Sinn Fein versus everyone else, with a 5:2 margin (notably including the Chairman's vote this time) ensuring the amendment was made, and the same margin carrying the motion as amended.

I had begun to wonder whether Dr Paisley's absence at the previous meeting had more to it than 'met the eye'. He didn't miss that many meetings, but this was the second in a row in which he'd avoided a controversial issue (the previous one being the Speaker's request for advice on cancelling his St Patrick's day reception). There was no doubt that Dr Paisley had access to plenty of political 'intelligence'. Had he removed himself from the firing line, so as not to have to face these difficult issues, and left George to do so?

If memory serves, George Savage might also have wondered out loud if that was the case. We clearly weren't the only ones to harbour suspicions on that front, since Dr Paisley felt it necessary, during the 11th of May meeting, to give a reason (which I don't recall) for his absence to members, and such explanations were not normally considered necessary.

John Dallat and PJ Bradley also felt the need (during the next meeting, on the 18th of May) to deny having participated in a 'walkout' from that evidence session. To be fair, their (separate) departures did not cause the loss of quorum, but I suspect they wanted to avoid any inconsistency with their party colleague's ministerial decision.

When the dust settled on that issue on the 11th of May, members got on with their normal business, which included what I assumed was going to be the usual 'nod through' of DARD's plans to make two Statutory Rules.

While members liked to be given their place as the Statutory Committee, and to hear from officials about the reasons for subordinate legislation, they usually went along with DARD's proposals without much bother. But they were surprisingly 'bolshy' about these ones, and, after a short discussion, members agreed (unanimously) that I should write to the Minister to say that the Committee disagreed with any measures that increased costs for farmers, and that they wanted to know what options DARD had explored to avoid such increases.

I was a little taken aback at their choosing this particular battle, as the proposed cost increases were relatively small, but I had my clear instructions, and a committee membership united behind them, so I did what I was told.

The next couple of meetings went by without much incident. The Committee had agreed not to meet on the 1st or 8th of June because of the 7th of June elections and there was a definite sense that members' minds were elsewhere. While the elections were not about Assembly seats, they were considered key barometers for the parties, particularly for the Ulster Unionists having gone into government with Sinn Fein.

There had already been a fair bit of 'positioning' from the Unionist parties, which had played out in the Assembly Chamber if not in the Committee itself. The First Minister, David Trimble, had made a personal statement on the 8th of May[34] to announce that he had lodged a letter with the Speaker resigning as First Minister on the 1st of July if the IRA had not decommissioned by then.

On the same day[35], the DUP had brought forward a motion of 'No Confidence' in the Sinn Fein Education Minister, Martin McGuinness (which, because of another valid Petition of Concern, was always destined to fall).

Both matters brought plenty of ill feeling, bouts of name-calling and spurious 'Points of Order'.

Things were relatively quiet in the Committee, though. The Minister's written briefing for the 18th of May confirmed no further outbreaks, no worrying suspect animals and no material being checked at the Pirbright laboratory[36]. While the Minister attended the meeting on the 25th to discuss FMD, it only took 30 minutes and was uncontentious.

Normal business was being conducted, but, at one point in the 25th of May meeting, the Committee lost its quorum for 25 minutes. This was unfortunate timing, since the DARD

---

[34] Official Report Bound Volume 11 pages 1-2
[35] Official Report Bound Volume 11 pages 24-42
[36] A research institute in Surrey dedicated to the study of infectious diseases in farm animals (Source: Wikipedia)

officials responsible for the disputed Statutory Rules were ready to come to the table.

While there were only four members present and the meeting was formally suspended, the Chairman suggested that it would save time if those members remaining held 'informal discussions' with the officials on the Statutory Rules, and that the Committee could come to its conclusions when again quorate.

Almost reverting to my risk-averse civil servant mode, I expressed a doubt about this being appropriate. To my surprise, Dr Paisley put a big arm around my shoulder and said, with a big grin: "Mister Clerk, I think I have been around this game a lot longer than you have". That was that. "Fair enough, Mister Chairman, you're the Chairman", I replied, and those members present went through the issues with the officials for the whole time that there was no quorum.

The Chairman waited until the end of the meeting, when there was both a quorum, and a decent balance of parties in the room, before returning to the 'informal' discussions. Those members who hadn't been present seemed quite happy to accept the reported views of those who had.

The Committee collectively agreed that they could not support the proposed regulations and that the Minister should be advised that it was the Committee's view that DARD should absorb the additional costs that had prompted the department to bring the regulations forward.

I ensured that all the post-meeting action points were carried out, then we were due a couple of weeks of relative Committee calm, before and after the elections took place.

It was during the Committee's election 'break' from meetings that my personal life almost crossed over with my professional one.

After a couple of years in a nursing home, suffering from dementia, my Mother died (in hospital) in the early hours of Wednesday the 6th of June, the day before the election.

It was a strange time, and her passing was actually a relief, as almost everyone rightly said at the time.

I even remember going ahead with picking up my new car (a family-friendly Renault Scenic) just a couple of hours after leaving my mother's remains at the Ulster Hospital. That sounds a bit heartless, but I had timed the pick-up for that week, since there were no meetings to plan for, and I couldn't be sure when I'd have the time again if I postponed.

Word (as it always seemed to) got back to Dr Paisley of my loss and I think it was Ian Junior who rang me on my mobile later that day to offer condolences. In conversation, he suggested that it was not unheard of (presumably at Westminster) for a Chairman to 'support' his Clerk by attending the funeral when such circumstances arose. Would I mind if the Chairman was able to attend my Mum's?

I was taken aback, but nonetheless touched, at the suggestion, then horrified in equal measure.

185

What sort of furore might Dr. Paisley's presence (complete with bodyguards) cause at Mum's 'regular' Presbyterian Church? And how would my brothers react, with them not being his biggest fans?

I'm not sure what I spluttered in response, but I probably put him off until the funeral arrangements had been made.

Fortunately, given the election on the 7th and the quickest death to funeral turnaround I'd ever experienced (Mum's funeral was held on Friday the 8th) Dr Paisley was not available to attend, and the dilemma did not need to be faced.

Phew!

Chapter 25: Dr Paisley rules the roost and leads the Committee in a 'Prayer'

The political landscape in Northern Ireland changed completely that June with the election results[37].

The DUP gained three of the eighteen Westminster seats, while the Ulster Unionists lost four. While the SDLP held their numbers, Sinn Fein gained two seats (although, true to their policy, they refused to take those up).

In the local elections, the DUP gained 40 Council seats while the UUP lost 31. Sinn Fein gained 34 seats with the SDLP losing three.

So, it was an understandably triumphant Dr Paisley who returned to the Chair for the Committee's meeting on the 15th of June. He came across as a completely changed man. Any concern he may have had that his working alongside Sinn Fein members might be electorally damaging to him or his party had, it seemed, been swept away in the euphoria of victory.

The DUP's tactics of working within the Institutions while continuing to oppose (and blame others for) them had paid off, and all the consequences of going into government with

---

[37] Source: Wikipedia

Sinn Fein were, it seemed, falling on David Trimble and his Ulster Unionist party.

In the Committee room there was almost a physical manifestation of this change. Dr Paisley was a big man, and always larger than life, but on this day, he appeared to fill the entire room.

He opened the meeting with a strident statement of intent that he wasn't going to be messed with. He had, he said, consulted with the Speaker, and he went on to set out his position, including his powers as Chairman of the Committee. He insisted that the conduct of Committee business should not be for outside discussion and threatened sanctions for any member who made his chairmanship a subject of external debate.

I hadn't been aware of his intention to flex his political 'muscles' in this way, so I was as gob-smacked as the rest of the Committee. But there wasn't a single word of dissent from any of them. Heads were lowered and eyes averted.

While Dr Paisley hadn't singled out any member as being a past culprit, my suspicions were that he was thinking particularly of John Dallat, who wasn't averse to a snipe or two about the Chairman in the press. I was relieved that John was an 'apology' for that day's meeting, and I wondered if that was really a coincidence.

I found the whole thing a little awkward but was content that his summation of Chairman's powers had been factually accurate, so I felt no inclination to interfere in his 'show of strength'. I also hoped that members would understand that I hadn't written any of this into the Chairman's brief, although I think that was probably clear enough from the look on my face!

With the Committee still sitting in stunned (almost) silence, the Minister attended to give what she hoped would be her last FMD update in person[38]. It was all positive news, with Northern Ireland's 'regionalization' status having been regained from the 5th of June, and no further outbreaks or suspects. Happily, controls were also being relaxed, with land and properties re-opening and a resumption of countryside pursuits such as angling.

This, the Minister reminded members, was in stark contrast to the position in Great Britain where restrictions remained firmly in place. There was tangible relief and, even among Unionist politicians, a realization that being able to take a Northern Ireland position, in co-operation with the rest of the Island's land mass, had been advantageous.

Shortly before the election, the Minister had reported to the Assembly that there had been a huge effort in terms of serology testing, with blood samples taken at that time from 170,000 sheep to meet EU requirements. A week on from the day's meeting, officials would report to the Committee that 300,000 sheep had been tested.

---

[38] See archived Minutes of Evidence (FMD) for the 15th of June

It was clear that there had been a serious mobilization of testing effort, which had involved private, as well as government, Vets.

So, at that day's meeting, there were many tributes paid by the Committee to the Minister and her staff for their efforts during the crisis, including one from the Chairman who said that DARD staff "deserved the thanks of the people".

Ian junior couldn't help himself but to add a caveat, insisting that "we" would still want to probe the department's handling of the crisis (he would later get his wish), while Gerry McHugh randomly asked the Minister if she would recognize Sean Clarke as Chair of a newly elected NIAPA Council (with her replying that the position had not yet been formally clarified).

The Minister concluded by saying that she was grateful to the Committee and, never ceasing to amaze me, Dr Paisley told her that he would "like to thank you personally for keeping me informed. It was appreciated".

The Minister looked as surprised as I felt, and thanked Dr Paisley for his comments. I suppose a successful election result allowed a bit of magnanimity, but I thought it was a statesman-like touch on the Chairman's part.

After the Minister had left, though, things were not quite so friendly towards the Minister's officials. Despite the Committee's representations, the Department had gone ahead with the Seed potatoes crop fees Statutory Rule, which had by now been made and laid before the Assembly. It was now the Committee's statutory responsibility to consider the Rule.

Not to go into too much boring legislative detail, this was a 'negative resolution' Statutory Rule, meaning that it automatically became law as soon as it was made. All the Committee could do, therefore, was consider it and have no objection, or table a motion for debate in the Assembly, seeking to have the Rule annulled.

I had researched this for the Committee, at the Chairman's request, and I explained to members that annulment of a negative resolution Instrument was a step that had very rarely, if ever, been taken in Westminster, on which the NI system was based. Nor had this been done by any other Assembly Committee since devolution, and I advised that it should not be taken lightly.

I wasn't sure that the Committee would want to take such a big step on what seemed a small issue. But in what might be described as a masterclass of troop-rallying, Dr Paisley made everyone, including PJ Bradley, convinced that they were protecting the small farmer against the mighty department and members formally agreed to recommend to the Assembly that the Statutory Rule be annulled.

Members then agreed the actual motion for tabling in the Business Office. I was interested to see how that would go down in Dundonald House.

The Committee also wanted to proceed with their sectoral Inquiries.

I had done quite a bit of work (along with Bertie) on the evidence taken so far in the Inquiry into the LMC. Now considered to be fully staffed as a Committee team, we weren't given the luxury of a specialist advisor for this subject. I therefore decided to check, with the Committee, my 'direction of travel' in terms of draft findings and recommendations, which I included in their meeting papers.

We hadn't really done that with the previous Inquiry reports, but it was my way of ensuring 'no surprises' when it came to the Committee's line by line consideration when a proper draft report was ready for them to consider. After a little bit of amendment and welcome direction from members, the Committee instructed me to proceed as planned.

I had also introduced, where time permitted, the practice of asking the Committee to agree the speaking notes that I had drafted, for the Chairman or Deputy Chairman, for those occasions when Committee business went before the full Assembly.

I was certain that this was the best practice to adopt, as it should avoid any accusation that the Committee's views weren't being properly represented. As part of this practice, I first ensured that the Chairman (or frequently Ian junior on his behalf) was content with the draft before it went to members.

This approach had worked fine for me so far, and, as one of the last pieces of business on the 15th of June, members readily agreed my draft notes for the Chairman's contribution to a 'Supply Resolution' (Departmental finances) debate on the coming Monday.

I was pleased at the way the Chairman and members had accepted me as their new Clerk, and how well they had responded to the subtle changes I had made to the way we did things.

It was a real buzz sitting next to the Chairman, and to be the 'Mister Clerk' that he asked to take members through the business of the day. In truth, I was quite proud of myself in having made the transition so (apparently) seamlessly to the next level. But you know what they say about pride…

The Committee's next meeting, on the 22nd of June, came three days after my 40th birthday, and the day before I was scheduled to enjoy my major 'Aussie barbie' themed birthday party in my back garden, a tradition started when I was 30, and which I can report was continued when I reached 50. So, all in all, I was in a pretty good mood.

Plenty of business was conducted in the first couple of hours, then George took over from the Chairman, who had other commitments to attend to and who had left the meeting.

It was shortly after he left that the draft minutes of the previous meeting were discussed, and this was slightly awkward for me, as I had to advise the Committee that the Chairman had asked for reference to his 'I'm in charge' statement to be added to that meeting's minutes. I hadn't included any reference in the draft minutes as it had seemed to me to be more like internal housekeeping than strictly

Committee business, but members were content enough for a reference to be inserted and they then approved them.

John Dallat appeared not to be in great form and he made a ratty point about 'people' referring, on the floor of the Assembly, to his 'ins and outs' (i.e., the record of his attendance at the Committee). John then insisted that his displeasure be recorded in the minutes of the current meeting. This made me all the more certain that John had been in Dr Paisley's 'sights' last week.

Once that was (thankfully) out of the way, we moved on to the draft speaking notes for the Chairman to use at the Assembly debate on the contentious Statutory Rule. The Committee's motion was called a 'Prayer of Annulment' (which was a Westminster term) and the debate was scheduled for Tuesday the 26th. The draft was handed out to Committee members on the day, my having agreed it with the Chairman in my pre-brief just before the start of the meeting.

I had based the speaking notes on members' discussions in previous meetings, and I included reference to members' disquiet at having had their views essentially ignored when the Minister decided to proceed with the Statutory Rule against their advice. I was expecting a quick nod-through as had been the case with speaking notes last week, but I misjudged that one badly.

John Dallat hit the roof, his face like thunder. I had never seen a member so angry. While his exact words were not recorded, I remember him saying something along the lines of: "That is

194

an outrageous personal attack on the Minister by Ian Paisley. We have had to deal with this man's tyranny for the last thirty years. I've had enough of it, and I'll not put up with it any longer!"

I could feel the blood draining from my face. All of a sudden, the Clerk's seat was a very lonely place to be. I had to bring this one back, and I knew it was time to shoulder responsibility. I calmly (though I'm sure my voice was shaky) said that it was I who drafted the speaking notes – the Chairman merely approved them.

This did not appease John, who started to turn his wrath towards me, saying that I shouldn't be 'attacking' the Minister. Apparently seeing an opportunity to wind John up even further, Ian junior jumped in to say "We have every confidence in the Clerk. Are you saying you don't?"

This could get out of hand, I thought. I had to do something, and quickly.

In my best conciliatory tone, I explained that because the motion aimed to strike down a piece of legislation, and was unprecedented in the Assembly, I had taken the view that the Chairman's speech needed to make a robust argument as to why the Assembly should annul it. I added that I was also reflecting the views expressed by members at the previous week's meeting at which, I acknowledged, John had not been present.

Having scanned the draft speaking notes again I saw that I'd used the words "The Minister" and "she" on two occasions and I suggested that if these were both changed to "the Department" then the points of argument could still be made but any sense of personal attack on the Minister (which had been completely unintended by me) would be lost.

Fortunately, John finally saw the draft for what it was, and not what he had thought it to be, and Ian junior backed off too, thankfully.

The other members were relieved at this de-escalation, and accepted it as a satisfactory resolution, signing off on the speaking notes with those amendments. The colour returned to my face and I took the Committee through the rest of the business without incident.

Once again, Dr Paisley had missed the controversy. Another coincidence?

I had one more thing I knew I needed to do, and after the meeting, I caught up with Ian junior and asked him for a quick word. We stood on the balcony overlooking the magnificent marble staircase that leads up from the Great Hall.

I told him that I understood that he may have felt the need to support me when I had come under attack from another member, but that I believed that the worst possible crime for a Committee Clerk in this Assembly would be that he or she was perceived to favour (or be favoured by) one side or the other. I said that while I appreciated having his (and his party's) confidence, I needed everyone's confidence, and I would appreciate it if he didn't use such a tactic to get at John (or anyone else) in the future.

Junior took this minor 'admonishment' well (actually I'm sure he didn't see it that way at all), and we talked about a few other things.

I suggested to him that, with a successful election behind the party, he and his Dad would be able to relax, and take it easy for a week or two. "Not at all", he said, explaining that his Dad had always taught him that you started fighting the next election the moment the results of the current one have been announced.

I'd never thought of it like that, but I saw how it was probably true, and it gave me, at that moment, some perspective on what being a politician might be like.

I went home that evening exhausted but pleased that I had defused a potential row (just call me Henry Kissinger, I thought) and that I had maintained (I hoped) my credibility with the Committee.

I also vowed to enjoy the next day's festivities, and I did. There was a cleverly designed cake, and much barbecue food and Australian beer were consumed, while I wore my stereotypically floppy hat with hanging corks. Cultural (mis)appropriation had not been heard of, back then (and while things may be different today I still have the hat).

After all that drama, the debate itself on the motion to annul (held on Tuesday the 26th)[39] was something of a disappointment. The Chairman used his amended speaking

---

[39] Official Report Bound Volume 11 pages 290-293

notes, but since the business Committee had only allocated 15 minutes to the debate, only four other Committee members spoke. The Minister opposed the motion (the only voice against) but it was carried without division.

So, history was very quietly made that day: the Seed Potatoes (Crop Fees) Regulations (Northern Ireland) 2001 (SR 2001 No. 228) were struck from the Statute Book. It may have been made quietly, but I was a little thrilled to have been part of it.

A couple of things of relevance came out of the Committee's last two meetings of the 2001/2001 session (held on the 29th of June and the 6th of July).

I had taken legal advice on the Committee's power to call for papers and convinced the Committee that the Minister's legal advice (on a fisheries matter) was privileged, and they could not require the Minister to hand it over. Members accepted my advice and (as that was the outstanding loose end on the matter) gave their agreement to DARD proceeding with a fishing vessel decommissioning scheme. That wasn't to be the last we'd hear of this scheme, however.

I also (with much misplaced optimism) handed out the first draft of the Committee's report on the LMC Inquiry in the vain hope that members might read it over the Summer recess.

You can lead a horse to water, as they say. Members probably felt they deserved a rest over the Summer.

I know that I did.

Part Three 2001/2002 – The End

Chapter 26: One day that would be remembered forever, other days we might wish to forget

The recess period allowed a summer family holiday (on a campsite in France, as I recall) and enabled me, pretty much at leisure, to do further work on the draft of the report on the LMC Inquiry.

I was also confirmed in my position as Clerk, having completed my six-month probationary period, with a Principal Clerk and the Clerk Assistant signing off my probation report.

Over the summer, Kyran had decided to seek pastures new, but the Agency had managed to place Easton back with us in time for the first meeting. It was good to have a familiar face, and one who already 'knew the ropes'.

It was a busy agenda for the first meeting back, on the 7th of September, and it included an appearance by the Minister. The purpose behind her attendance was, I suppose, to provide reassurance to members that everything in the Foot and Mouth 'garden' was still rosy in Northern Ireland. Members seemed happy with what she said.

The Minister also put forward the suggestion of one Friday date in each of the next three months for her to appear before the Committee. As usual, I had 'pre-sold' that suggestion to the Chairman after further discussions with the Minister's PS and this caused no difficulties for either him or any of the members.

I had also drawn up a draft forward work programme for the Committee, based on matters in which I knew members were still interested, matters outstanding from the 2000/2001 session, and things I knew that the department had coming our way.

Two senior officials came to the meeting to lay out further departmental priorities, and this allowed on-the-spot editing of my programme to give a good indication of what the Committee would be covering up to mid-November, and which members were content to agree.

Prioritisation was crucial. There was so much 'bumf' that had come into the office over the Summer for the Committee's attention and, ever mindful that I could withdraw none of it without their being made aware, I went through each subject as quickly as I could.

By this stage, I often provided members with a copy of the cover letter or document title page only. My aim was to stay within the requirements of Standing Orders, but also to avoid members taking an undue interest in matters which, frankly, were not very important, and which would take up their valuable time (and make my team's work harder).

In every such case, I made it clear that the full source material was available in the Committee office if any member wished to see it. As before, I expected that my staff would not be knocked down in the rush, and they weren't.

There had been quite a few Statutory Rules laid during the summer recess and I reminded the Chairman to seek declarations of interest before the Committee formally considered them.

Fortunately, none of the long list of SRs considered that day sought to increase fees payable by farmers, so they were easily dealt with. All the other business of the day was also concluded without incident, leaving staff with the usual round of tidying up points from the meeting just held and preparing papers for the next one. We were firmly back on the treadmill again.

Outside the Committee room, the political mood music wasn't great. The First Minister's resignation had taken effect on the 1st of July, and this had necessitated a 'technical' suspension of the Assembly by the Secretary of State for one day on the 11th of August, which allowed the Executive to keep going with an acting First Minister.

The first serious plenary debate of the year took place on Monday the 10th of September. The debate was prompted by some of the most distressing and disgraceful scenes ever witnessed, even given Northern Ireland's troubled past, when children aged between four and eleven, and their parents, were seemingly forced to run a gauntlet of loyalist hatred, daily, to reach their Primary School (Holy Cross) in North Belfast.

Surely no-one who had seen the TV footage of those scenes, with the bricks, bottles, and angry sectarian screaming in the faces of frightened children, could possibly justify what had gone on?

I listened to the debate with interest from my team's semi-open plan room. Over the summer, I had been given my own 'space' in another office on the same floor - part of a larger room with a divider between me and some typists – but there was more life about the main room, so I spent a fair bit of time there.

Gerry Kelly, from Sinn Fein, had tabled the motion and led the debate as a local MLA, which was a red rag for some members to begin with, given his IRA connections. And while most of the MLAs who spoke in the debate condemned these vile acts against children, many did so while also indulging in the usual 'whataboutery' argument (what about this murder, what about that intimidation that 'your side' inflicted on 'our side' and so on and so on).

This meant that the waters of the debate's intended message were completely muddied. I shook my head, wondering what it would take for these Members to 'rise above' the expected tribal response.

It wasn't an edifying debate, and I was glad there was not enough plenary business for an Assembly sitting on the Tuesday morning to distract me from my work, since we had papers to get out by Tuesday afternoon for Friday the 14th's meeting.

Tuesday the 11th started as a normal day, and I think I might even have got out for a walk at lunchtime in the beautiful grounds of Parliament Buildings, which are among the nicest in Belfast, certainly in the government's estate.

But shortly after finishing that walk, everything changed in my, and in everyone else's, world.

I had dandered round once more to the team's office space, only to be met by all of the team, and several others from the fourth floor, gathered round our small monitor/tv. I joined them and watched, aghast, at repeated images of a plane flying into the second tower at the World Trade Centre in New York, while the first tower was in flames following its earlier hit. (From memory, we didn't see pictures of the first plane hitting its tower until a couple of days later.)

This 'breaking news' event had, of course, taken over all tv coverage but it was initially difficult to hear the 'commentary' from the news anchors over the gasps and general hubbub as more and more staff came, or were pulled, over to watch. It seemed, though, that two crashes at the same site must be deliberate, and the realization dawned that this was an attack, rather than an accident. Then word filtered through on the TV about an explosion at the Pentagon in Washington.

We watched on, motionless, and the hubbub in the room reduced to barely a word. All thoughts of issuing papers and Committee meetings were forgotten among our anguished thoughts for those inside the towers, and in the planes, particularly as we realized there must be people alive in the intact floors of the towers above where the impacts had taken place. How and when will they be reached, we wondered.

Everyone who watched those events live will have their own experience firmly embedded in their memories. I expect mine was the same as many others', but I will maintain until the day I die that I felt a physical change in the air around me at about 3pm that day, as one of the towers spectacularly, and completely, collapsed in full view of the watching world. I immediately thought of Obi Wan's description of having felt a "great disturbance in the force" just as a planet was destroyed in Star Wars, one of my favourite movies. I am certain I felt it that day.

The tower's collapse added a further layer of shock on top of what we'd already witnessed – from there being a burning building with hundreds, perhaps thousands, of souls awaiting rescue to literally nothing but dust. And half an hour later, the other tower suffered the same fate exactly.

This was becoming too much for many of the staff, and our bosses at the Assembly simply said that everyone who wanted should just go home. I made sure the team packed everything up and suggested we come back the next day to see where we were, where the world was. We were completely numbed and ashen-faced as we left the building.

I returned to work on the Wednesday worn out, as most people were, from watching the wall-to-wall coverage of events on TV, events which had included a fourth hijacked plane that didn't reach its target.

205

For the next couple of days, I had the irrational (as I now see it) concern that Parliament Buildings might itself come under attack. It was the seat of our government, and a very easy building to find from the air. Why wouldn't it be a target? I was honestly frightened just being inside the building. Everyone was completely on edge, so I reckon my thoughts were understandable given the horrors of that fateful day.

I have no recollection of the conversation, but I must have contacted either Dr Paisley or his son and agreed that the Friday Committee meeting should be postponed until the following Monday. One of us must also have made the arrangements to book a room and move the catering order from one day to the next, but we were all in a daze.

Business Office colleagues had been making arrangements too. The Acting First Minister (Sir Reg Empey) and the deputy First Minister had tabled a motion of condolence for the Assembly to debate at the earliest possible time, and the debate had been quickly scheduled for Thursday the 13th.

The team and I had to catch up with work for the re-arranged Committee meeting, so I watched the debate on the same little TV where we'd watched Tuesday's events. This time, I thought, they're all going to come together. This is bigger than any differences that our local politicians might have.

206

It was clear from the outset that I was very much mistaken. Before the debate even got underway[40], Dr Paisley managed to put on record that he'd tabled an amendment to the condolence motion, with the Speaker immediately shutting him down by saying that he would not then, nor would he in future, allow such an amendment to be debated.

From there, it only got worse. While much of Sir Reg Empey's contribution condemned the acts of terrorism perpetrated on the American people, and extended Northern Ireland's deepest sympathy to them, he also compared the IRA's attack in Canary Wharf to the US attacks, saying that they differed only in scale. The tone was firmly set.

Dr Paisley swept in next with a highly charged and emotional speech decrying any dialogue with terrorism and alleging that concessions to terrorists had "turned the monster into a greater monster".

He wasted no time in saying that there were Members in the Chamber whose organization was part of the international organization that carried out the attacks. Furthermore, he led his DUP colleagues in walking out of the Chamber, in order not to hear the contribution of the Sinn Fein President, Gerry Adams.

Some of the remaining Party leaders tried to bring the debate back to its subject, and to articulate what most of us were

[40] Official Report Bound Volume 12 pages 41-45 (this section of the Bound Volume notably includes a black border around the text to signify its subject of condolence)

probably thinking. But to no avail, when a further diatribe from one of my (North Down) constituency MLAs, Bob McCartney, included an opportunist accusation against Gerry Adams, alleging that he had held a position in the Belfast Brigade of the IRA when it blew apart the bodies of 11 people on 'Bloody Friday'.

The Speaker had had enough, and cut him off, saying (I thought memorably) that "most of us are aware that more words spoken do not necessarily mean more condolences expressed. It is time to express our condolences in ways other than words". He then 'put the question' (on the debate's motion) which was agreed without challenge and indicated that a Book of Condolence would be opened for Members (and Assembly staff) to pay their respects.

I think that much of my respect for Dr Paisley (and he had proven very worthy of respect as a Committee Chair) was lost that day.

The 'walkout' must have been a calculated political move on his part. It earned many headlines and I'm sure gained nods of approval from many people, particularly those who had suffered at the hands of the IRA. It may even have helped the Party on its way to becoming the biggest party in Unionism, but for me, it was just plain wrong to subvert the expression of condolence in the way that he and his party colleagues did.

I queued to sign the Book of Condolence with a heart that was heavy - not just with the effects of the recent atrocity, but with my own sense of hopelessness that the Assembly would ever really work.

Chapter 27: Back to business (but does any of it really matter)?

The re-arranged Committee meeting on Monday the 17th of September came and went.

Business was conducted in a strange, quiet and sombre mood, and there was paragraph by paragraph consideration of my latest draft LMC Inquiry report, which was half-hearted, at best.

There was a threat of the Assembly's suspension in the air once more, and a plenary debate on paramilitary activity was scheduled the following day (which would no doubt create further divisions) and, frankly, I wasn't sure that any of it mattered a jot, given what had just happened.

I couldn't, however, allow my personal feelings to get in the way of my professional responsibilities, and I also had a team to lead so I simply tried to get on with it.

In the meeting on Friday the 21st, the Committee (in closed session) got into the nitty gritty of the LMC report. Members were more 'hands-on' with this than the previous three reports, and I had a delicate balancing act to perform: reminding them of evidence they'd heard, trying to steer them away from contention within the Committee, and basically thinking on my feet to come up with solutions to meet their needs.

In this activity, and in many other sessions throughout my time as 'Mister Clerk', I used to subtly seek input from the member whom I privately called my 'voice of reason': David Ford from the Alliance Party.

If I thought that members were becoming too partisan, or struggling to reach agreement on a point, I'd suggest some middle line and glance over to try to catch David's eye, with what I hoped was a 'please come in and help me' expression.

We never spoke openly about this tactic, but I have little doubt that David was aware of what I was doing. In fairness, David very rarely let me down when he got 'the glance', and I was convinced that his endorsement added credibility to my interventions in the eyes of the members who knew he was not on either of their 'sides'.

There had, over the summer, been a centrally agreed change in how Statutory Committee reports were to be handled by the Assembly. Rather than releasing a report to the public, waiting for a department's response and then seeking to debate and secure the Assembly's endorsement of it, the new plan was to have the Assembly 'take note' of each report immediately.

The intention was, I think, to give the Assembly its rightful place, meaning that the report was released to MLAs first, and only sent to stakeholders and the wider public after the Assembly had taken note. I had briefed Dr Paisley on this change immediately before the meeting and he asked me to explain it to the Committee members, who were happy enough.

The fishermen 'hadn't gone away, you know', and ANIFPO gave their views to the Committee again during the 21st of September meeting, on the subject of vessel decommissioning.

The ANIFPO delegation was immediately followed by two DARD fisheries officials: Jim (whom I knew well) and Peter (whom I didn't). They seemed to have formed a settled team for attending Committee briefings and members' familiarity with them seemed to help.

In particular, Jim (the more senior official at Grade 7 level) pleased the Committee when he agreed to recommend to the Minister two changes to the proposed measures in the fishing vessels decommissioning scheme. Those changes had been suggested by ANIFPO and members had thought them reasonable and practical.

I think this outcome helped a little in regard to my internal turmoil and loss of 'faith' in that the Committee's work in this area appeared to have had a positive effect.

Unfortunately, such outcomes didn't really happen often enough for my liking. Much of the work appeared to have no effect at all, and my overall feeling of unease was becoming one of disillusionment.

I thought that a lack of focus in the Committee may be part of the problem. I was becoming concerned that members had developed a tendency to hear about a subject, then ask for DARD officials to appear before the Committee to explain it to them, even if it was a low priority, uncontentious, subject.

I had put many innocuous papers and reports in front of members, suggesting (and fully expecting) that they should simply be noted. But quite frequently members gave a "we need to get officials up to brief us about that" response, without any real consideration of what might be achieved. I had also started to notice that the Chairman was one of the worst culprits for this.

I understood that he and members would not want to be accused of failing to identify and follow up on an important matter, especially if that matter had, in whatever format, been brought to their attention. But I was confident of my own judgement on what was and wasn't crucial for the Committee's work, and I felt that the Chairman and members should in turn be relying on my judgement. I hadn't let them down yet.

I also believed that this resulted in a very inefficient use of members' (and DARD officials') time. There was more than enough business to be conducted in a weekly Committee meeting without unnecessary add-ons.

So, I decided to be proactive, first securing the Chairman's, then members', agreement (at the meeting held on the 5th of

October) to ask for written updates on most occasions rather than the default being a request for officials to attend.

That felt like a win. I knew that it would also earn me the gratitude of the Department's Assembly Liaison Officer (the DALO) who was also called Paul. I think Paul had been promoted to Deputy Principal from the same DARD promotion board list on which my name had appeared. I had some previous dealings with him, and I had a lot of time for him. We were keenly aware that this approach would help at both ends.

That 5th of October meeting was to be Easton's last as an Agency worker on my team (he'd found something else, he said) and the Agency supplied us with another admin support worker called Niamh, who worked her first Committee meeting on the 12th of October, when George Savage took the Chair in Dr Paisley's absence.

In that meeting, the Minister gave a further update on FMD (all good news, still) and informed the Committee that there was going to be an independent investigation into the FMD outbreak.

In between those two Committee meetings, on the 10th of October, the Assembly 'Take Note' debate was held on the Committee's LMC report. The circumstances surrounding that debate just added to my sense of unease, since it felt like two political worlds were co-existing, but incompatible.

Committee business continued, with Dr Paisley generally deploying a fair and reasonable chairmanship style which ensured that meetings were conducted in a business-like fashion, and with noticeably much less sniping than before the Summer.

In contrast, Assembly plenary business seemingly lurched from one fractious debate to another. For example, the day before the Committee's LMC report was debated there were two motions debated in plenary (one of which had been tabled by Dr Paisley) which aimed to exclude Sinn Fein from holding ministerial office.

The first motion stated that there was no confidence in Sinn Fein as it was not "committed to non-violence and exclusively peaceful and democratic means" while the second referred to the IRA's "failure to offer up its illegal weaponry for destruction"[41].

Such motions were required, according to the legislation, to be carried by cross-community support and since they didn't have the support of the largest nationalist political party, both were doomed to fail. You can imagine the tenor of debate, however.

There had been a further one day technical suspension of the Assembly on the 22nd of September[42], which had allowed it to limp on again with an Acting First Minister.

But with the exclusion motions having failed, ministerial resignations were now expected from both the UUP and the

---

[41] Official Report Bound Volume 12 pages 287-306 and 321-334
[42] 'History of the Assembly' on NI Assembly website

DUP, so there seemed to be little hope of the Assembly's survival.

Yet a day later, I was back in the Officials' box, listening to members agreeing how important it was for the Committee's 33 recommendations on the LMC to be implemented[43]. It was difficult to reconcile these two political worlds as forming part of the same Institution, and that did nothing for my overall mood.

During the LMC debate, I looked on from the Box as the Chairman and Deputy Chairman 'tag-teamed' the speaking notes I had prepared for them (covering several of the most important issues), while all but two of the other members also contributed.

I found myself nodding in agreement as Ian Junior wondered aloud whether the current report would suffer the same fate as the previous three, with important matters being considered and then "nothing else appears to happen". Had that been sanctioned by his father, I wondered? Was Dr Paisley also beginning to have doubts about the Committee's role?

Ian Junior went on to question the point of the Executive at all, citing the very few Bills that had been introduced in the Assembly since devolution. I had begun to have similar thoughts myself, as my confidence in the institution waned.

Anyway, as expected, and following the Minister's undertaking to respond in due course, the Assembly 'took

---

[43] Official Report Bound Volume 12 pages 341-352

note' of the Committee's report without any problem so another box was ticked for the team, and we all returned to our meetings in the more familiar territory of Committee Room 135.

Dr Paisley had got into the habit of asking the most junior Committee staff member for a cup of tea at the very start of each Committee meeting, and Niamh (pronounced 'Neeve' for those who may not know) was quickly lined up for this task when the Committee met on the 19th of October.

When Niamh was introduced to him, Dr Paisley guffawed, saying "Ah, Niamh, I hope you're not naïve!" and his shoulders shook with mirth at his own wit, before adding his usual: "get me a cup of tea please, dear".

It was hardly the funniest gag anyone had ever heard, but clearly it was a keeper, as Dr Paisley repeated it at every subsequent Committee meeting Niamh attended, and I would try to catch Niamh's eye as the punchline was delivered, in an effort to distance myself from this feeble humour. As I recall, Niamh wasn't overly happy at the tea-making practice (or, perhaps, the comedy turn), and, after just five meetings, she'd had enough and moved on.

Not much went on during the Committee meetings on the 19th and 26th of October, and there was no meeting on the 2nd of November, as we were in the Halloween recess (which offered a short respite from the treadmill).

I missed the next meeting on the 9th, although I can't recall why. A Clerking colleague called Sheila sat in for me that day, when members agreed my draft speaking notes for the Deputy Chairman's use in a plenary debate the following Tuesday, notes that he delivered without incident.

Outside the Committee room, there was, finally, some significant political progress, with the IRA having put some weapons 'beyond use' in October and with David Trimble being re-elected as First Minister on the 5th of November (along with Mark Durkan as deputy First Minister).

That should have lifted my mood somewhat. But, to me, the last couple of months had gone by in a bit of a blur really, with the 9-11 attack still very fresh in my mind.

I think that made it hard for me to remain convinced that what we were doing was terribly important in the wider scheme of things.

Chapter 28: George finally gets his junket

The meeting on the 16th of November was uncontentious. The Minister briefed members about the forthcoming December Fisheries Council and the main aim of reinstating the 10% cut to the Nephrops Total Allowable Catch (TAC) figure (cue my internalized Paisley impersonations of him saying 'Knee-Frawwps').

The Committee also heard that the Minister was now recognizing Sean Clarke as NIAPA Chair and had agreed to take that organisation's representations once more. I expected the Committee to do the same and I wondered if members would be embarrassed about the way Mr. Clarke had been treated, when next he appeared before them.

John Dallat brought a favourite hobby horse out for a bit of further exercise, again raising the issue of notes being passed to Dr Paisley from the gallery while the Minister was appearing before the Committee. On this occasion, Dr Paisley explained that the note had been a private one from a member of his staff, but John insisted that I raise it once more with my senior management.

At the following week's meeting (on the 23rd), I reported that the Clerk Assistant's response was that the public were, through new written 'Gallery Rules', being discouraged from passing notes. It was acknowledged, however, that while regular Committee members could nip outside to speak to members of the public, the Chairman could not do so quite so easily, so the final decision on the issue would lie with the Chairman.

While enjoying his partial victory, John wasn't happy with the Chairman having the final say, and he said he might approach the Speaker on the matter. I'm not sure whether he did or did not, but I don't think the issue was ever heard of again.

Having lost Niamh (John for now taking up the tea-making duties) we were down to a team of three, but we soldiered on.

I was playing a careful game of trying to provide a good service while avoiding us being overwhelmed, and I therefore did my best to deflect members' suggestions for yet further Committee Inquiries. They were, unfortunately, an inquiring bunch, and members suggested bank charges, rural tourism and the Foot and Mouth outbreak (from guess who?) as possible topics.

I had found it difficult to manage two Inquiries at once, in conjunction with all the regular business, and I strongly encouraged the Chairman to encourage the Committee to complete the Rural Development Programme Inquiry before staring the next one. He sort of agreed with me but at the same time was keen for the Committee to be seen to be working hard, so I knew that 'one at a time' was going to be a hard sell.

The Committee's continued interest in fisheries matters was also about to add to my workload.

Early in the meeting on the 7th of December the Minister, with Jim (the Fisheries Grade 7) sat alongside her, explained that the European Commission were proposing even further cuts in the TAC in the Irish sea and that this was contrary to scientific advice.

The Minister said she was seeking support from the Irish and British fisheries Ministers at the upcoming Fisheries Council meeting, as the local fishing industry could in no way sustain such a cut.

The Producers' groups' early and continued lobbying of the Committee was now paying off, with members seemingly pretty outraged at what they were hearing and badly wanting to help.

I expect that any Committee Chair other than Dr Paisley would have ordered a stiff letter to be sent to the Commission voicing the Committee's dismay and support for the NI Industry. But our Chairman was sure he could go one better, and, at his suggestion, the Committee resolved to seek a meeting with European Union's Commissioner for Agriculture, Rural Development and Fisheries, Franz Fischler.

Given the European dimension, the Committee further agreed that they should do so by arrangement with the three Northern Ireland MEPs.

Looking around the room that day, I felt that some of the members were quietly impressed with this idea, and quietly hopeful that the Chairman, as an MEP with plenty of European connections, could pull it off.

Members also quickly agreed that, if a meeting could be arranged, the Committee should be represented by the Chairman and by George Savage and PJ Bradley. At last! A possible junket for George!

Later that day, another member (I think it was John Dallat who had joined the meeting late) queried the make-up of the delegation, suggesting that it wasn't sufficiently 'cross-community' (being 2:1 in favour of the Unionists).

The Chairman's response was very persuasive: that it would be appropriate for the two holders of the offices of Chair and Deputy Chair to attend, along with the Committee member with the greatest MLA constituency interest (in this case that was clearly PJ). The Chairman also doubted if a larger delegation would be accommodated by the Commissioner.

Faced with such a compelling argument, John indicated that he was content, and no further words of dissent were heard.

While also impressed by the ambition of seeking a meeting with Fischler, I was, frankly, petrified at the thought of accompanying a Committee delegation, as their Clerk, to a meeting overseas.

I was, however, relieved that the hardest part of the exercise – getting the Commissioner's agreement to a meeting and liaison with the other two MEPs – was going to be looked after by Dr Paisley's people. I wouldn't have known where to start!

After the Committee meeting, I had to swiftly draw up (and agree with him) a letter from the Chairman that would form part of the approach to the Commissioner.

I then asked the Assembly's travel team (for by then we had such a team in place) to look at possible arrangements for the four of us to go to Strasbourg, where the European Parliament was due to meet the following week and where Commissioner Fischler could therefore be found.

We were about to go international!

Chapter 29: Boys on tour

Sure enough, it wasn't long before word came through from Dr Paisley's office that a meeting slot had been agreed with Commissioner Fischler, that Jim Nicholson and John Hume had been informed, and that they both had been invited to a pre-meeting over lunch at the European Parliament. That was impressive.

The travel team also moved quickly to finalize our arrangements. It was at such short notice that every single hotel room in or close to Strasbourg had been taken, and we were booked into a hotel in Baden Baden, across the border in Germany, some 75 km from Strasbourg airport and 60 km from the Parliament Building.

To be honest, I don't recall the exact timings of the scheduled trip, but I know that Dr Paisley spoke as Committee Chair in the Plenary debate on the Programme for Government early in the afternoon of Monday the 10th of December. So, I'm pretty sure that three of us (George, PJ and I) headed off in a taxi from Parliament Buildings to Belfast City Airport later that afternoon, with Dr Paisley close behind in his police-driven vehicle.

A new terminal had opened that June at the City, and this was probably my first experience of flying out of it, so I couldn't help but feel a little excited. It was exciting, too, to be in the presence of such a recognizable individual in such a public place.

There was nudging and pointing at our group by almost everyone in the airport, and many greetings (all friendly) called out as we strode towards the Gate. With the two other MLAs, 'Mister Clerk' and the two bodyguards very much looking like the big man's entourage, this was my first little taste of the celebrity lifestyle.

The role of the two RUC officers finished at the Gate and the remaining four of us boarded the aircraft (in Business Class for the first time in my life). Whether by accident or design, Dr Paisley and I were sat together in the front row (I was pleasantly surprised to find the middle seat of three being left free and useable as a tray) while George and PJ were in the row behind.

No sooner were we airborne than the stewardess (as we called them then) offered us Bucks Fizz and snacks. Dr Paisley declined 'the Devil's buttermilk' in favour of water, while I enthusiastically accepted mine. The imp in me wondered how well it would go down if I asked for Dr Paisley's Bucks Fizz as well. I didn't dare do that, of course, but I wasn't about to let the upgraded opportunity go to waste and gratefully took a second glass when the stewardess offered it.

There was very little conversation out of the Chairman on the short flight to Gatwick. He was clearly very used to travel, and to using the time fruitfully to catch up on work: I got the impression that it was spiritual, rather than political, matters that he was attending to, so I was equally happy to leave him to it.

I was busy trying to work out quite how I was going to pay what might be an expensive taxi fare at the Strasbourg end of the journey. I had been furnished with a Committee Credit Card (which was also quite exciting since my own was, like everyone else's I knew, 'maxed out' to the low credit limit that was responsibly given by banks at the time). But was it likely that a card could be used for a taxi? I thought not.

I had also been supplied with a small wadge of euros by the travel team. Euros were still a relatively recent 'invention', and I'd used some on holiday in France, but they certainly made it less of an issue that our hotel was in a different country to the Parliament.

We disembarked the aircraft at Gatwick and were met by two rather unfriendly plain clothed police officers, who clearly weren't terribly happy with their short assignment. They insisted on whisking Dr Paisley off to a car for the very short journey between terminals. The rest of us were left to fend for ourselves as normal 'punters', but his journey to the other terminal probably took longer than ours.

I had certainly noticed a difference in the 'Paisley effect' between Belfast and Gatwick. This time, there was only the odd 'whisper and point', as much, probably, at his being met by two officers as anything else. But he was still being recognized by some fellow passengers, and that added to the fun I was having with the whole trip.

226

I remember little enough about the next leg of the trip, from Gatwick to Strasbourg. Dr Paisley continued to work, and I enjoyed the perks and delights of a better class of travel than I was used to. I was clearly not going to let myself get to the stage where I was noticeably 'under the influence' – I was technically still 'on duty' - but equally I thought it a shame to turn down anything that was 'free'. My lack of abstinence didn't seem to bother the Chairman either.

As for George and PJ? I didn't really pay much attention to either during the journey, other than to make sure we all stayed close together between flights, as I did not want to be losing an MLA on my watch. From what I knew of them, I suspected that George had more affinity with Dr Paisley's approach to the availability of a free drink and that PJ had a greater affinity with mine!

On landing at Strasbourg and retrieving our small amounts of luggage, we were met by no-one at all. Either the pond had got considerably larger, or the fish had got considerably smaller. No-one elbowed their neighbour and pointed our way either. Let's face it, the airport was probably full of MEPs arriving from all over Europe, and these passengers were probably more interested in their self-importance than with anyone else's.

During the layover at Gatwick, the four of us had made a tentative plan. Dr Paisley needed to go and 'sign in' at the Parliament (presumably to ensure payment of the generous expenses due to MEPs). He was happy to do that, and as an MEP, he'd be reimbursed his taxi fare to the Parliament

227

Building. We had agreed that the rest of us would sort out our own taxi for the trip to Baden Baden, and Dr Paisley would catch up with us later at the hotel.

That had seemed a reasonable idea in Gatwick, but as Dr Paisley started to make his way to the taxi area, George approached me, and expressed his concern at us leaving "the Doc" to make his way to the hotel himself, saying something like: "The man is well into his seventies".

This level of concern for a political opponent (albeit a fellow Unionist) pleasantly surprised me, even after his helping hand in Kilkeel, and on reflection I thought George was right. The risk of losing a member on my watch would be significantly increased if we separated.

After a further conflab with the Chairman, we decided that the rest of us would hitch a ride to the Parliament Building in Dr Paisley's taxi, then find our way from there to the hotel as one group. Like many best-laid plans, however, this one went slightly awry.

The first part went fine, though our taxi driver's driving style suggested he didn't know (or care) about how much any of us would be missed by our families if we didn't come home. Then, after Dr Paisley had secured his 'signing-in' fee, he asked Parliament staff to order us a taxi for the 60km to Baden Baden. That was, I reckon, shortly before 8pm. We waited, and waited, and repeatedly checked with the reception staff, then waited and waited some more.

228

Whether it was French drivers being unhappy about the German destination, I don't know, but, whatever the reason, a taxi didn't come for us until well after midnight, and we weren't in our rooms (we each had our own, of course) until close to 2am. Not ideal, with a relatively early start in the morning to get back to Strasbourg for the meeting with Commissioner Fischler. Most of my euros went on the taxi fare.

We were all, by that stage, starving too, and I remember ringing round the rooms assuring the members that I would pick up the tab for room service through my Committee credit card. Actually, I wasn't sure about my spending powers, but I was happy I could justify the expense in these circumstances. Even though it felt much too late to be eating, I managed a (rather overpriced) club sandwich and then it was time for sleep.

Bright and early the next morning, I made my way down to the restaurant for breakfast. Dr Paisley had already been shown to a table for the four of us and had just sat down. Breakfast was served at the table, rather than buffet-style, and the nice waitress greeted us with a very friendly "Good morning" and asked us what we would like to order.

Ignoring the printed menu, Dr Paisley roared "I'll have a bowl of porridge, dear!" In her slightly accented English, the waitress replied that she was sorry but that the hotel had no porridge. "No porridge? That's why you're such a weak country" bellowed Dr Paisley, as heads turned throughout the breakfast room. I thought he was joking. Of course he was

229

joking. Wasn't he? What next? Would he actually mention the war?

He let out a big guffaw, the waitress smiled, and I let out a very big sigh of relief that a major diplomatic incident with 'the Germans' had been avoided. We duly ordered cooked breakfasts from the menu and the waitress scurried off to let the kitchen know.

"I'll have some tea, please, Paul" said the big man next. I was taken aback, not at the tea delivery expectation, which was by now something of a team in-joke, but by him remembering and using my name. This didn't happen often, and never in front of other members, when "Mister Clerk" was the norm. I supposed he felt he couldn't call me "dear".

So, I may have been slightly distracted as I went to the tea station, took a teabag from its packaging, placed it in a very nice little teapot and poured in the hot water from the still. I was having black coffee, as was my wont, and brought both back to the table. Dr Paisley allowed his pot to brew for a while, then poured the tea into his white cup, where its bright red colour stood out, and a very fruity berried aroma filled the air. Whoops!

"Whaaaat? I'll not be drinking that, Mister Clerk" roared Dr Paisley. "Indeed not, Chairman, for that is not tea at all" said I, and I scuttled off to find another teapot and a proper English breakfast tea to put in it this time. If my Clerking capabilities were being judged on my tea-making, I'm afraid I'd just lost a lot of Clerking points in the Chairman's eyes, and he took great comedic pleasure in regaling George and PJ with the story of my heinous crime, as they arrived (separately) at the table.

Breakfast over, and with best suits on, we gathered at the hotel reception, where, thankfully, Germanic efficiency and the Committee credit card saw a taxi arrive within five minutes of ordering, and whisk the four of us, safely and comfortably, to the European Parliament Building in Strasbourg.

I am slightly hazy on the day's itinerary, but we definitely took a bit of a tour of the building as I remember looking around the Parliament's debating chamber, with its semi-circular rows of seating. There was a lot of buzz about the place, and I found it an interesting scale-up from the small debating chamber at Stormont.

Our group met up with the Ulster Unionist MEP, Jim Nicholson, for a short pre-briefing. Jim had been an MEP for about 12 years by that stage. That was well short of Dr Paisley, who had been there around ten years more than that, but Jim was very experienced none the less.

According to Jim, the SDLP MEP, John Hume, was not going to join us. I don't recall any particular reason being passed on, but I think Dr Paisley was disappointed that the full complement of Northern Ireland's MEPs wasn't going to be able to present a united front to the Commissioner. So was I. I could have seen through him staying away if the delegation had been briefing against the SDLP Minister's position in some way, but our group was actually here in support of it.

In any event, Dr Paisley shared the Committee's letter with Jim, a letter which Dr P was going to hand-deliver to the Commissioner that afternoon. I was on hand to remind the Chairman and explain to Jim about the background to that letter – matters that the Fish Producers and the Minister had reported to the Committee, and the members' reaction to them.

In the main, though, I stayed, quite rightly, in the background as the elected representatives did their thing. The key issue, everyone agreed, was reinstatement of the 10% cut in the TAC for Nephrops, and avoidance of a further cut.

The pre-meeting with Jim shifted to more salubrious surroundings as we moved into the MEPs' dining room. It was lovely, all white tablecloths and smart waiting staff, and with one empty seat at the table we enjoyed a delicious starter and main course. Discussions continued, and were going well, with the tactics for meeting Commissioner Fischler agreed.

Then I stuck my big foot in it. Jim Nicholson asked if anyone else fancied dessert, since he most certainly did (I think there may have been a particular favourite of his available that day). Looking back, I can't quite believe my response: "Oh yes, please – now that I'm here I might as well stick my snout in the trough too". You know the expression: 'he had a face like thunder'? Jim's face was exactly that, plus one or two other weather systems as well.

I immediately knew that I'd made a serious error of judgement with a man I'd just met for the first time, and that I had clearly hit a nerve. I'm sure he had been on the end of countless accusations of being aboard the (very lucrative) EU gravy train. But here he was, enjoying a working lunch, only to have a jumped-up Assembly official 'putting the boot in' with his throw-away line.

Jim could barely get his words out, so incandescent was he. I think that: "work extremely hard", "long hours", "legitimate expenses" were all phrases that I caught amidst his tirade.

I was mortified, which was clear to anyone close enough to see my face, which was by now the colour of the Chairman's morning tea. All I could do was apologise and say that I had meant nothing personal by my comment.

That was true, in that I was not getting at Jim personally, although I was of the opinion that the European Parliament was a colossally wasteful institution. I thought this was exemplified by moving the whole shooting match from Brussels to Strasbourg several times per year for meetings of the Parliament, and I did take the view that membership of the Parliament was a fairly cushy, and extremely lucrative, number as far as politics went.

Perhaps Dr Paisley was more used to me and my sense of humour. He might even have quietly enjoyed Jim's (and my) discomfort. Whatever the case, my comment was like 'water off a duck's back' to him and he didn't (thankfully) seem at all bothered by it.

233

George and PJ just stayed quiet, and I was concerned that Jim's outburst may have embarrassed them somewhat. That annoyed me more than upsetting the MEP: I'd probably never see Jim again, but I had to have the confidence of the Committee members in all of my abilities, including my judgement, and my comment had been very ill-judged.

When things seemed to have settled down, and with what can only be described as a brass neck, I went ahead and ordered dessert (and coffee, to boot). Jim had his dessert, though he didn't seem to enjoy it that much, and the rest of the meal was, let's say, quieter than the earlier courses had been.

After a bit of freshening up, and sitting about, it was time for us to meet Commissioner Fischler, a bearded gentleman who seemed friendly and who made the group feel very welcome.

The Commissioner listened attentively to the case being made (all four of 'our' politicians participating well in the discussions) but he always seemed to have a counter argument against the points being raised.

Discussions turned to the previous 10% cut in the nephrops TAC, and our 'team' laid it on pretty thick about the damage that would be done to the industry, how it could not possibly be sustainable if the original cuts were sustained or additional cuts made, and how such cuts could not be justified by the science.

The Commissioner appeared very relaxed throughout this heartfelt appeal. Then, in what seemed like a planned move, an official approached him and whispered in his ear. With a nod, he then delivered his coup de grace.

This was along the lines of: "From what I understand, the fishermen in Northern Ireland did not declare that they reached their Total Allowable Catch for nephrops last year". He went on to suggest that something similar had happened in (I think it was) the last five years, quoting figures for their declared catch, which more than suggested that the 10% cut (and even further cuts) should do no damage at all.

How the wind suddenly went out of the group's collective sails. Dr Paisley looked round desperately to me, clearly hoping that I'd have some clever rebuttal for this revelation. I had none. The delegation had been done up like the proverbial kipper.

There was always a suspicion among some that fishermen might not fully declare all of their catch all of the time, and the department had fisheries inspectors whose job it was to try to ensure that they did. But whatever the truth of that matter was, Fischler was using the officially declared figures, and the local fishermen had not seen the fatal hole that this put in their argument.

Politicians do not want to leave any meeting with their tails between their legs, but this group got as close to doing just that as I'd ever come across. Dr Paisley was raging outside the meeting room, mostly annoyed, I think, that the Fish Producers' Groups had put him in a position where he had appeared to be foolish and ill-informed.

To be fair to him (and as a surprise to me) his first thought was to tip the Minister off about Fischler's information, and he instructed me to talk to her PS as soon as possible to make sure she was aware of it before she attended the December Fisheries Council meeting.

Formal business over, we had a little time left before heading to the airport. Jim Nicholson returned to his hard, and apparently thankless, work. Dr Paisley stayed at the Parliament Building to do whatever else MEPs did, and the rest of us went (separately) to have a look at the delights of Strasbourg itself. I had visited there briefly in 1981 when I inter-railed around Europe with two friends, but my only real (and very happy) recollection was that the Strasbourg youth hostel had served cold beer, when very few of the hostels we stayed in had served any beer at all.

It wasn't long before it was time to make our way back to the Parliament, and although we hadn't planned it, I actually met George and PJ in the centre of Strasbourg – they had taken a look at some of the sights together, it turned out. While I was happy to walk back, the members insisted on us taking a taxi.

There followed one of the most excruciating (but fortunately short) journeys I had ever suffered, with the two members speaking their regional dialect English to a driver who had very little English, with both doing the archetypally English-speaker thing of just repeating themselves more loudly when he didn't understand. My schoolboy French deserted me completely as I attempted to translate in both directions.

It also slightly bothered me that George and PJ seemed intent on putting down Strasbourg's buildings and its river by comparing them unfavourably with Northern Ireland's. But it was all very light-hearted, and the driver seemed to understand that from their tone if nothing else.

We met up with Dr Paisley again at the Parliament, got another taxi to the airport and started the return journey. There wasn't much craic at all on the way back. There was a bit of deflation among us all about how things had gone but (in the strange world that politicians must live in) there was also a certain level of satisfaction that they'd at least be seen to have done what they could to help the local industry.

I enjoyed a nice glass of wine with my in-flight meal while Dr Paisley sat beside me, bible open, clearly working on a future sermon for his flock.

On our final return to Belfast, it was apparent again that the 'pond' was smaller and the fish much bigger, and, with a cheery wave to some more admirers, Dr Paisley headed off with his on-duty CPOs and I headed home.

I was exhausted but very pleased to have got everyone home safe from our boys' tour of Europe.

Chapter 30: Armstrong takes one small step

Our wee trip must have taken it out of the three travelling Committee members, or perhaps it was the lack of a tour 'victory' to recount, but none of the three turned up at the next Committee meeting on the 14th of December, the last scheduled before Christmas. Indeed, only five members showed up at all.

Not only that, but staff were thin on the ground too. Easton made a fleeting (one meeting) comeback from the Agency, since we still hadn't got a replacement for (the far from) 'Naïve Niamh', and John was also missing that week.

The absence of the three delegation members caused a bit of an issue, and one which I hadn't previously had to address, in that it meant that neither the Chairman nor Deputy Chairman was present. Who, then, would chair the meeting?

I think I must have previously considered the possibility of such an occurrence and researched what happened in other legislatures in those circumstances. I may also have had a day's notice that the Chairman and deputy Chairman would be absent. In any event, I was prepared and able to guide the members in what they needed to do, with a high degree of confidence that I was telling them the right thing.

238

This involved me symbolically (and also physically) taking the Chair. As a non-MLA, that just felt (and probably looked) wrong, but my formal position as the Committee's Clerk made it technically ok.

I remember feeling a little additional buzz when placing my rear end in the seat where the big man's normally rested, as I asked the members present for nominations of a member to be Acting Chairperson. With only five of them in their seats, meaning that the Committee was only just quorate, that could have been very interesting.

To my surprise, Boyd Douglas immediately nominated Billy Armstrong, and the other members unanimously agreed that he should take the Chair. I was pretty sure, from their expressions and reactions during our meetings, that Billy wasn't always taken seriously by the other members, but perhaps that made him the ideal candidate – someone who they could be sure wouldn't make things too complicated while briefly performing the role.

I'm certain that Billy saw his nomination and 'election' in a more positive light, though, and he was beaming as he stepped forward to take the seat that I had now vacated.

I handed Billy the day's 'Chairman's brief' and said, quietly, "Just follow this and ask me to take members through the business and you'll be grand". He did, and he was, though in fairness the business was not contentious at all.

In the absence of any of the delegation to Strasbourg, members accepted a written note of the meeting with Fischler that I had cobbled together and instructed me to send it to the Minister to warn her of the Commissioner's 'bombshell'. In reality, I'd already spoken to the Minister's PS and the DALO as soon as I'd got back to the office.

The five members were as displeased with the Strasbourg meeting's outcome as the delegation had been. At every briefing they'd given the Committee, the Fish Producers Organisations had indicated that their nephrops TAC was not nearly enough as it currently stood, and that a further cut would be catastrophic. Elected representatives hate nothing more than being made a fool of, and they were not happy with this at all.

Members were, however, much happier to learn that on a recently discussed topic (the Beef National Envelope) the Minister had agreed to follow the recommendations that the Committee had made to her.

And so it was, with members enjoying at least some small sense of purpose and achievement, that Billy brought his first (and last) meeting as Acting Chairperson to a close and wished everyone a happy Christmas.

Chapter 31: What's another year?

Fully recharged after over a month since the last meeting, we prepared for the first meeting back on the 18th of January 2002.

I had secured the services of Roberta as our administrative support, so the team was up to full strength again. But what would this year hold for us all?

The Minister had been expected to attend and brief the Committee, but a rescheduled Executive meeting meant that she could not, and no alternative date was offered before the scheduled meeting in February.

Neither the Chairman, nor members, seemed overly bothered by this – I think that the early 'push and pull' dynamic had been replaced with a healthy Committee respect for her workload and a realization on her part that the Committee had a legitimate (and constructive) role to play. Or perhaps the novelty had simply worn off somewhat.

DARD fisheries officials attended to report the outcome of the December Fisheries Council meeting. It was, as always, not a great result for the fishermen, but not as bad as it might have been. That 'threaten a lot, and they'll settle for some' approach was a clear and frequently used tactic on the part of the European Commission, it seemed to me.

The officials tried (unsuccessfully) to explain why the Nephrops TAC had not been officially reached in the previous years, but the focus seemed now to be more on the Cod Recovery Plan and the closures of fisheries that were now required.

There was some discussion on compensation for fishermen who would now have to tie up their boats. Committee members supported the call for compensation, but the officials appeared to be suggesting that this was not going to be the Department's policy so members decided they would need to see the Minister after all, and Dr Paisley charged me with setting up a meeting for her to attend.

In other business, Ian Junior (who was nothing if not persistent) once again proposed a Committee Inquiry into the Foot and Mouth outbreak. He must have worn the other members down and they agreed to consider terms of reference for such an Inquiry the following week. Great!

I had done quite a lot of work on the Rural Development Inquiry over the Christmas recess, and I wanted to bring a draft report to members as soon as I could. I was, however, very anxious about the potential for a conflict of interest to be perceived in relation to my having worked in Rural Development so relatively recently.

I therefore embarked on the grandest piece of 'ass-covering' Clerking that I'd ever done (or ever did). As the Committee reached the relevant agenda item, I declared an interest and (I thought dramatically) withdrew from the meeting. I had

242

arranged for Joe Reynolds (who was by then the Principal Clerk of Committees) to take my place in the Clerk's seat and explain to members my difficulty, and my proposed solution to it.

If members agreed, Joe explained, he would act as an independent assessor of my draft findings, conclusions and recommendations, and (hopefully) provide assurance that these were entirely objective and based solely on the evidence that had been placed before the Committee.

I was pleased to learn from Joe afterwards (and from the minutes drafted by Bertie, which I equally studiously did not play any part in approving) that members had unanimously expressed their confidence in me, and that they had commended my approach to the issue.

I'm sure most of them, as Councillors or MLAs, had been accused of some conflict of interest or other in their day, so they could probably see that this offered protection for them, as well as for me. That said, I took satisfaction in the fact that, at least on this occasion, my judgement was considered to be sound.

The meeting on the 25th of January was uneventful. I had issued draft outline findings for the Rural Development Inquiry ahead of the meeting, but it was painfully clear to me that no-one had bothered to read them. Members didn't admit that, of course, and I was instructed to proceed with the first draft of the report, on the basis that members would approach me individually if they had any issues with the outline findings. Not much chance of that, I assumed.

Members also instructed me to find out more about the Department's (independent) review of the FMD outbreak before drafting terms of reference for a Committee Inquiry.

The Committee then conducted the extra meeting with the Minister about the Cod Recovery Plan (on Monday the 28th of January). She was adamant that there wasn't a great case for a compensatory 'tie up' scheme for the Cod recovery Plan but agreed to speak to her relevant ministerial colleague about the prospects of social security payments for fishermen who could no longer ply their trade. That seemed to satisfy members at least in part.

The first meeting in February (on the 1st) was noteworthy only in relation to the Committee's decision to proceed with an Inquiry into Foot and Mouth, and I sought members' direction on methodology, press notices and the terms of reference themselves.

There must also have been some 'back-channels' approaches to me through the DALO, as I raised DARD's concern about the possible implications for DARD staff being called to give evidence to the Inquiry (presumably in relation to matters such as investigations into farmers' wrong-doing, and in relation to decisions taken by individuals).

Unsurprisingly, members were not too concerned about the consequences of their Inquiry for Civil Servants, but they instructed me to take legal advice on the application of the

Committee's statutory powers to call for 'persons and papers' in such circumstances. The Chairman, in particular, often referred to those powers and I got the sense that he was itching to exercise them.

In other business, a DARD official attended and assured members that a couple of Statutory Rules proposed by the Department would address recommendations that the Committee had made in its retailing report. My goodness! It seemed that the Committee's report hadn't just been left to gather dust, as Ian Junior had complained. That particular legislation was, needless to say, quickly nodded through by members.

On the same day, members heard a litany of problems and complaints from the 'Potato men'. I loved that the Committee called them that, and it prompted (in me) visions of the Toy Story character (Mr. Potato Head) every time they appeared before the Committee. The Potato Men's view was that a new European policy spelt serious trouble for them (but didn't it always, I thought).

The European dimension sounded very familiar, though, and I was relieved that the Committee's decision, after deliberation, was for me to draft a letter to Commissioner Fischler (who was also Agriculture Commissioner) which Dr Paisley could hand deliver at a meeting he had already scheduled with him as an MEP.

No Committee delegation would be sent to meet him this time, thank goodness. No more fruity tea or snout-in-trough disasters for me, or Commissioner ambushes for the members!

It was probably around this time, although I can't be certain of the date, that an incident occurred which I took as a demonstration of Gardiner Kane's standing with his party leader.

The Committee was in the middle of a meeting, with the usual mix of officials and sectoral interests in attendance. Gardiner was in his usual place, which was to my left and close to our end of the Committee table. He leaned closer to me and whispered that he needed the loo.

He had, however, looked around and realized that if he left, the Committee's quorum would be lost, so he wanted to know if the Chairman would suspend the meeting for a 'comfort break'. Dr Paisley had done this on a number of occasions, usually when he needed to relieve himself.

I duly passed this request on to the Chairman, on my right, but was surprised when he said "No, I don't want to interrupt the meeting". That was that. As time went by, and no other member joined the meeting to ensure the quorum, Gardiner became more and more distressed. He appealed directly: "Doctor Paisley, I really need to go!"

But to no avail. Not only would the Chairman not suspend the meeting, but he made it clear to Gardiner that he should stay where he was, in order to avoid the loss of quorum.

I was appalled, seeing how much discomfort Gardiner was in, and I lobbied the Chairman on his behalf several more times. It wasn't even as if we were in the middle of an important presentation at that point, so business could easily have waited. What had Gardiner done to deserve this, I wondered? And is he so scared of his leader that he is prepared to wet himself, rather than defy him?

It was a good twenty to twenty-five minutes later that Dr Paisley finally suspended the Committee meeting for a break, and it seemed that he did so only because he needed the loo himself. Fortunately, there was a gent's toilet almost next door to Committee room 135, and Gardiner beat him to it with a sprint worthy of Dwain Chambers.

I was shocked by Dr Paisley's demonstration of power and control over a party 'underling', which could surely only be described as bullying, and I'm afraid he went even further down in my estimation that day.

Chapter 32: The Grand Old Duke of York

In life, there are moments when a decision, however small it might seem, changes everything. I made one such decision for the meeting on the 8th of February.

I can't actually recall why I wanted a Friday off. Somewhere in my head there's a suspicion that it might have been golf-related, but on the face of it, that seems unlikely, given the time of year. In any event, I arranged cover (a Clerk called Damien, who had been appointed at the same time as I had been promoted, kindly agreed to take the meeting) and cleared it with Dr Paisley and my line management that I could take leave that day.

The agenda was entirely innocuous, and I had anticipated that it all would go smoothly and easily for Damien. I'm afraid it did not.

My return on the Monday was met with reports of a members' meltdown, prompted by allegations made by fisheries representatives about the behaviour of two DARD Fisheries officials. This had, apparently, resulted in an instruction that a letter be sent to the department requiring the officials to come before the Committee and answer the allegations.

I thought "Whoa! What on earth happened?"

I spoke to Damien, who was a bit shell shocked by the whole thing, and then asked the Assembly IT team to let me hear the private tape recording of the meeting. At that time, all meetings that were not recorded for the Official Report were recorded by equipment in the room (with members' knowledge, but not for external use).

On the tape, I could hear that several pieces of regular business were conducted without incident. Francie Molloy had found that his Chairmanship of the Finance Committee was taking most of his time and Sinn Fein had replaced him on our Committee with Mick Murphy, who attended his first meeting that day. With the DUP's stance on Sinn Fein unchanged, it had been left to Damien to inform the Committee of the change.

The Committee team also had a newbie on show, Jonathan, who was to replace Roberta as our Agency admin support officer from the following week, and he was introduced to the members.

The Committee also agreed my draft conclusions (so far) for the Rural Development Inquiry report, took evidence from DARD officials that would further inform that Inquiry, made a couple of technical amendments to the terms of reference for the FMD Inquiry, and discussed further easements of FMD controls. Members also heard that the Chairman's scheduled meeting with Fischler hadn't taken place, but that the Committee's letter had been sent by fax. All was going perfectly well.

249

The problems arose when the two Fish Producers Organisations came to the table to update the Committee. I had known they were coming, but I had no reason to believe that their presentations would go any differently to all the other fisheries briefings that they had delivered.

Dick James and some colleagues from NIFPO were up first. They were fairly measured in their argument but indicated that the Cod Recovery Plan would cause fishermen at least a 40% loss in earnings and stressed that there was a need for a compensation scheme, which it seemed that DARD was not keen to pursue. That didn't seem to cause too much contention, but it proved to be just the warm-up.

Alan McCulla and his team from ANIFPO came to the table next and immediately went on the attack. I had no idea what prompted such a change in their tone. They had previously been somewhat critical of DARD, but they had always seemed to accept that the officials were trying their best.

This time, ANIFPO came up with a long list of complaints about the fishing vessels decommissioning scheme and about two DARD officials in particular (Jim and Peter, who were no strangers to the Committee).

Alan had said that he had no confidence in these officials and alleged that they had been unhelpful to the fishermen, and to the Committee. More specifically he stated that the officials had, through errors and omissions, misled the Committee about the scheme. Worse still, he alleged that the officials had bragged about misleading the Committee, saying that members would not, in any event, be able to understand what they were being told.

Even through the hiss of the less-than-clear tape recording I could feel the tension mounting in the room as this went on. Poor Damien, I thought. Not only did he not know anything about the fishermen, the DARD officials or the scheme they were talking about, but nor did he have access that day to what might have been a 'voice of reason', as David Ford was not present at the meeting.

What I heard next on the tape was an object lesson from Dr Paisley in rabble-rousing. In a very short space of time, he had every one of the members (Republican, Unionist and Nationalist) up to (as my Mother used to say) 'high doe'.

He cajoled members and encouraged their anger, reinforcing their initial surprise and annoyance with loud articulation of his own shock and outrage. This went on until the Committee was, to a man, completely furious and (metaphorically) demanding the heads of these officials. The only thing missing in the room, it seemed, was a supply of pitchforks and torches.

Dr Paisley had, in less than five minutes, truly marched them all to the 'top of the hill'. I got a sense, in that moment, of how he had garnered so many followers and successfully opposed so many things. He was very good at this: here was a master at work.

I can't say for sure that I would have been able to head this 'group hysteria' off at the pass had I been in the room that

251

morning, but I might have been able to at least sow some seeds of caution about the claims, which seemed to be lacking in any detail. I would also have offered to forensically examine DARD's papers on the decommissioning scheme on members' behalf, to confirm what had and had not been said to the Committee.

In terms of the allegations, I suspected that either, or both, of the officials might well have privately made disparaging remarks about the Committee and/or some of its members. Heck, if you saw members in action, it would be hard not to be critical of some, and of their grasp of certain subjects. I just couldn't envisage either official doing so in front of key stakeholders. Nor, frankly, did I think any official in his right mind would set out to deliberately mislead a Statutory Committee.

But the die had apparently been cast with the Committee's instruction to draft a letter to the Department, and I mulled over Bertie's first draft in the context of his notes (and Damien's story) from the meeting, having listened to the tape.

I will admit that I used my absence from the meeting as a reason for delaying the issue of this letter – saying that I needed to confirm that its contents were what members really wanted. What I also did was to get straight on to the DALO, to warn him what was about to come the Department's way.

I knew this could get messy, but I hoped it could be resolved without too much pain, and we quickly organized a meeting between the Chair and Deputy Chair and the Minister and her senior officials for the following day.

Unfortunately, this meeting didn't help, inasmuch as the DARD folk admitted that there had been a mistake in the guidance that it had issued to fishermen in relation to the decommissioning scheme. This part-confirmation of the fishermen's allegations served only to fire up the Chairman further. He (and, he was keen to point out, the rest of the members) needed answers.

The Department team hadn't had much time to think through the ramifications, but they suggested that any Committee meeting with the named officials would need to be in private session, and that senior DARD officials would need to accompany them (Peter was a relatively junior Staff Officer, while Jim was a Grade 7, which wasn't considered a senior management grade either).

Dr Paisley agreed to leave it that the Committee would consider its proposed letter during the meeting on Friday the 15th of February. I had bought myself a little time.

Having re-read some of the previous correspondence just ahead of that meeting, I thought I might be starting to understand why the fishermen's representatives had become so upset and had 'lashed out' at DARD.

Not only was there to be no tie-up compensation relating to the Cod Recovery Plan, but it seemed that DARD officials had refused to play ball with how the fishermen wanted to 'game' the decommissioning scheme.

253

ANIFPO had written to the Committee to ask members to 'sponsor' a change they wanted made to one specific regulation in the Statutory Rule through which the decommissioning scheme would be implemented. This, incidentally, was an SR which the Committee had previously (and formally) agreed.

What ANIFPO sought was the removal of a requirement that the recipient of a decommissioning grant must not purchase another vessel within ten years of the grant.

I had no sympathy at all for this request, and I could see why DARD was against it.

It seemed that fishermen wanted to be paid (very handsomely) from public monies to leave the fishing industry (an industry in which they argued they couldn't make money), as part of a scheme which had the stated aim of reducing fleet numbers and therefore mitigating the issue of over-fishing. But at the same time were the fishermen now insisting that they should, in the near future, be able to buy another boat and return to the industry?

What a 'have your cake and eat it' cheek, I thought, and I'll admit that, for once, my personal views influenced my advice to members on the day of the meeting. I suggested that they should instruct me to reply that the Committee was not empowered to make or amend subordinate legislation.

That was, in itself, true, but I offered up no possibility that the Committee might consider the matter further or try to influence the department to consider such a change. Members accepted my (biased) advice and instructed me to reply as I had suggested.

Having secured that outcome, I suggested that the Committee might wish to approach the Minister on some of the other points the fishermen had raised, such as differences between Northern Ireland and GB schemes, and the mechanism that would be used to consider the fishermen's bids for decommissioning grants. Members agreed.

After all that preamble, the meeting moved on to consideration of the draft letter to the Minister about the Committee having been misled or misinformed by DARD staff. By then I had softened the tone of the letter considerably from that which might have issued on the 'day of Damien', and my draft sought to confirm the tentative compromise proposals for a private session and an invitation to senior officials to observe.

Although they were still being 'egged on' by the Chairman, with the wind in his sails from the Minister's admission that there was an error in the guidance, members bought into the softened letter ok, and to my suggestion that the Committee should also write to ANIFPO to seek more specific detail around their allegations.

I ensured that both letters were issued soon after the meeting ended. In doing so, I was acutely aware that I could possibly be accused of leading the Committee down a certain path on these matters, rather than strictly following orders, but I felt it was part of my role to protect members from doing something they might regret.

One thing that should, perhaps, have brought perspective to these discussions was the news that morning that a Kilkeel fishing boat was missing at sea. The outlook for those aboard was not good, and I remember thinking at the time that there were much harder and more dangerous places to work than the inside of a Committee room.

At the next meeting (on the 22nd of February) the Minister confirmed details of the terrible tragedy that had befallen a prawn fishing boat from Kilkeel, the 'Tullaghmurry Lass'. Three generations of the Greene family, all of whom (including an eight-year-old boy) were called Michael, had been lost at sea and, despite a huge search effort, no bodies, nor the vessel, had yet been found[44].

I hoped that this terrible event might dull the Committee's appetite for conflict over the allegations about the DARD officials. But I could also see how it may have prompted some of the members to feel that they should 'take up the cudgels' for fishermen at this time.

After having been updated on the tragedy, the Committee went into closed session with the Minister and her Special

---

[44]The wreck of the vessel was found, with bodies still on board, over a month later (source: Belfast Telegraph (online) article of 4 February 2017, reporting on the funeral of Mrs Anne Greene, who lost her husband, son and grandson in the tragedy)

Advisor (better known as a 'SPAD'), a move that required the public seating area to be cleared.

The Minister advised the Committee that DARD had launched its own investigation into the officials' conduct as a result of the Committee's letter. She then suggested that the Committee might wish to wait the outcome of that investigation before deciding on what to do next.

That suggestion might have been better received had she not then demanded sight of the Committee's correspondence with the FPOs on the subject, adding that such correspondence "would be discoverable".

The Chairman did not pass up the opportunity for conflict that this offered and, to be fair, her tone and use of the legal term had raised the hackles of a number of other members too. Dr Paisley immediately countered, quite forcefully, that Committee correspondence with stakeholders would be confidential until and unless members agreed to it being made available to DARD.

Once the Minister had left, members agreed not to delay their request to meet the officials, and they approved the issue of a further letter asking the officials to appear at the following week's meeting (on the 1st of March). They also instructed me to take legal advice on the confidentiality of Committee correspondence, in order to confirm whether or not the Chairman's line could be held successfully.

By the 1st of March meeting, Joe Reynolds, freshly promoted to the role of 'Clerk Assistant', had provided the Committee with his report on his examination of my work on the Rural development Inquiry. In his report, Joe gave the Committee all the assurances that I had felt were necessary, and members were content that this allowed them to formally consider my draft findings and conclusions. Another one ticked off.

Much of the day's interest, however, was focused on the issue of the DARD officials. A letter from the Minister had been received shortly before the meeting had started, and it was accompanied by a report following DARD's investigation into the allegations that ANIFPO had made.

Members felt that they didn't have time to consider the Minister's report that day and determined that they'd meet again on the following Tuesday to discuss it. The Chairman suspended proceedings briefly to allow me to make enquiries about room availability and within a few minutes he was able to set a date for meeting at 2pm on Tuesday the 5th of March in a different Committee room.

I also provided members with the advice from the Assembly's Legal Advisor about confidentiality of correspondence (and associated advice about matters 'sub-judice' which he had included). Following the Committee's deliberations, I was charged with drafting a further letter to the Minister summing up that advice.

There wasn't much time until the next meeting, but there was sufficient time for me to identify that an annex to the Department's investigation report included a copy of legal advice obtained by the Department. Sight of that legal advice had previously been the subject of a request from the Committee, a request denied by the Department! I thought this quite amusing, as did members when I pointed it out to them.

They were not so amused when I mentioned that the contents of the advice appeared inconsistent with what the Minister had said to the Committee at the time (May 2001).

While the issue itself was 'past the post' I thought that members would want to know. On reflection, I suppose this may have fomented mistrust and influenced members' thinking on the current DARD/Committee dynamic.

While noting that the DARD 'investigation' report hadn't identified any particular wrongdoing by the two fisheries officials, members agreed that they believed it was still reasonable and appropriate to want to speak to the officials themselves, in order that they might reach their own conclusions on the matter.

I was therefore instructed to get yet another letter off to the Minister asking her to make the officials available on the 8th of March (i.e., three days later) in private session, again with the option of being accompanied by senior officials. The Minister was asked to respond by the 7th.

With plenty of continued prompting from the Chairman, members simply weren't for letting this one go. Such a flurry of correspondence! I could barely keep up.

Dr Paisley had also asked me to brush up on my knowledge and understanding of the relevant provisions in the 1998 Northern Ireland Act and the associated Assembly Standing Orders.

I had done that ahead of the meeting and, at his behest, I reminded members that Statutory Committees had a statutory power (i.e., a power enshrined in law) to call for persons and papers and that a refusal to attend (or provide papers) could result in a formal notice being given to that person (such notice to be given by the Speaker). Ultimately the formal notice could be legally enforced, and I could see the Chairman was getting more and more interested in this device.

I had also, as promised to members when this whole thing had begun, forensically examined the exchanges between DARD and the Committee about the decommissioning scheme. I reported that I had not found anything concrete to support the allegations, nor had ANIFPO provided anything further by way of detail.

What I had spotted, however, was that DARD's investigation report had referenced information on the calculation of a 'Strike Price' having been supplied to the Committee.

'Strike Price' was a technical term about how bids made by vessel owners would be considered by the department. It was not a straightforward system, but it was crucial to anyone's understanding of how the scheme would operate. The Strike Price mechanism had also been mentioned in ANIFPO's allegations about the Committee having been misled.

When I checked the Committee's records, I found that a fax we had received on that topic was incomplete (a page was missing). This wasn't an easy 'spot' unless you looked very closely, and no-one had noticed at the time.

There was no way of knowing whether the page had been missed at the Department's end or the Committee's, but I thought it would be ironic if all this hassle was being caused by a single missing page. The Committee instructed me to bring this to DARD's attention and to secure the missing information.

After further deliberation, the Committee gave me an instruction that the letter to the Minister should include a threat that, should the officials not make themselves available, the Committee would, reluctantly, approach the Speaker asking him to give formal notice in accordance with the Committee's power to call persons and papers.

I really didn't think that the allegations were serious enough, or had enough supporting evidence, to go down the formal statutory route for 'calling for persons', and I made this clear to members. But, again strongly encouraged by the Chairman, some of the members felt that this was an issue on which the Committee should not back down.

This threat was a massive escalation, in my view, and it didn't make for comfortable discussions with the DALO after the meeting had concluded. I had my instructions, however, and this time I carried them out (albeit reluctantly) to the letter.

Chapter 33: Someone is always watching

By way of background to this 'aside', I should declare that, as a former DARD official myself, I knew Jim, one of the two Fisheries officials embroiled in this dispute, personally.

We wouldn't have regarded ourselves as friends by any means, and nor had we worked directly together to any great extent. But Jim was a well-known 'character' in DARD and we got on pretty well whenever our paths crossed.

That made it uncomfortable for me to hear the allegation that he had deliberately misled the Committee and, from what I knew of him, I was pretty sure that would never have been his intention. And I remained certain that while he may well have been disparaging about certain Committee members when chatting to colleagues, he would never have said as much to ANIFPO officials.

Life, as they say, goes on, and at the same time as this dispute was ongoing, I popped into Jim's office (in an annex, really a hut, in the Stormont Estate) for a personal visit. It was Jim's birthday that day and, as was customary at the time, there was a 'bun worry' for him, aimed at colleagues who wanted to pass on their birthday wishes.

I don't remember everything about this visit, but I suspect that, given Jim's 'character' status, there was probably wine on offer, as well as the usual tea and coffee, and it wasn't unusual in those days for Civil Servants to have an occasional drink during working hours.

Never one to miss out on a free bun (or a glass of wine, for that matter) I and another former colleague spent 30 minutes or so wishing Jim many happy returns and indulging in the home-made delights that his team had supplied.

I don't recall the exact date – I had never celebrated his birthday before – but what I do recall is that the next time I met Dr Paisley in his party room to discuss Committee business, he said to me something like: "Would it be true, Mister Clerk, that you went to see one of the DARD fisheries officials that's in trouble with us?"

I explained that I had simply been wishing a former colleague happy birthday and assured him that there had been no mention made of the dispute or of Jim's part in it. In short, I sought to reassure him that I had nothing to hide.

Inside I was, however, a bit shocked and annoyed at Dr Paisley's inference (as I saw it) that I might, somehow, be 'fraternizing with the enemy', and therefore acting against his and the Committee's interests.

I was also taken aback that Dr Paisley's 'sphere of influence' extended, apparently, to having spies in the fisheries Annex, but that, I suppose, was just me being naïve. He hadn't got to where he was without the help of many supporters. It was a lesson learned, however, and one not forgotten.

The whole episode made me feel that my integrity and loyalty were, perhaps, being questioned, and I realized I was becoming less and less comfortable in my relationship with Dr Paisley.

Chapter 34: Local and International diplomacy in very short supply

The meeting on the 8th of March came around very quickly.

As may have been expected, the Minister had ignored the Committee's deadline on the fisheries matter, with no officials appearing that day. She did, however, provide another letter in response, which only arrived after the meeting was underway.

The Committee took note of the Minister's letter, which was sticking to the line that DARD wanted to manage its own staff and that the officials wouldn't be made available to the Committee.

In accordance with the Committee's previous decisions, I had drafted, and the Chairman had forwarded, a submission to the Speaker asking him to give DARD formal notice and calling for the DARD officials to attend.

My next instruction was to draft a further letter from the Chairman, to let DARD know that he had written his submission to the Speaker and that he was awaiting the Speaker's response.

I could hardly believe it had come to this, when there seemed to be so little substance behind the allegations, and it seemed to me that there was a danger of this becoming a 'pissing contest' between the Chairman and the Minister.

I knew I wasn't the first person that felt they had no choice other than to 'follow orders' but I was by now finding it really difficult to carry out instructions with which I clearly didn't agree.

I suspected then, and confirmed much later, that some former colleagues in DARD felt that I was driving the Committee's actions in this dispute, or at least encouraging them, and that I was acting as some sort of disaffected former employee. I really was not doing any such thing, but I was concerned how all this might affect my future if and when I returned to the Department after my secondment was over.

Timing was also now going to be an issue in getting this thing resolved. St Patrick's day was fast approaching, and this was always a very busy period for local politicians, with many crossing the Atlantic to attend Washington events.

The Chairman indicated that he would not be available on Friday the 15th. The Deputy Chairman also thought he may have to go to Brussels on or around that date, while several other members thought it likely they too would have other engagements - so many, in fact, that members agreed to postpone the next meeting until the 22nd of March. Easter was just round the corner as well, and, along with it, the Assembly's Easter recess.

That was the context in which I then sought members' views on a potential, and separate, problem, this time with an international dimension.

At the previous week's meeting (1ˢᵗ of March), I had alerted members that some Canadian politicians were due to be in Northern Ireland in a couple of weeks, as part of a visit organized by the Department. They were a delegation from the Parliament of Canada's Senate Standing Committee on Agriculture and Forestry. Members had agreed that they would be content to meet the visitors, and to provide a lunch for them if that was appropriate.

The official recently appointed as Principal Clerk of Committees (John) was in charge of what was called the 'overseas office' and it had been he who had (on the 26ᵗʰ of February) copied me into his email exchange with a DARD official in which it was reported that the Canadians had expressed an interest in meeting our Committee.

I had subsequently passed on the Committee's offer to the same DARD official but had heard nothing back by way of confirmation or formal request. Immediately before the 8ᵗʰ of March meeting, however, a Clerking colleague (Peter, who had lived in Canada and had a personal friendship with the Senate Committee Clerk) tipped me off that the delegation's confirmed programme for the visit included a reception and lunch to be hosted by our Committee on Friday the 15ᵗʰ.

I asked members what they wanted me to do.

The Chairman was concerned that, with the Committee meeting scheduled for that day already having been postponed, it was unlikely that the Committee could offer any sort of decent 'turnout' for such an event (assuming that a formal request to host it would eventually be made by DARD).

Members agreed that a poor turnout might appear discourteous to their Canadian counterparts and concluded that the Committee should convey its regrets that it was now unable to facilitate such an event.

While I agreed that it would be better to cancel than have no-one turn up, I was uncomfortable at letting foreign visitors down after the offer had been made. So, after the meeting was over, I had a quick word with colleagues in the Speaker's office, then suggested to the Clerk's office that the Clerk (Arthur Moir, the head of the entire secretariat) could host a lunch for them.

I made some provisional arrangements around catering and emailed John, who had gone home by that time, to ask the overseas office to take over the arrangements for this visit.

Early on the following Monday (the 11th), John received my message and rang me straight away. I was no great fan of John's, as it seemed to me that he did very little 'front-line' work with MLAs, compared to the rest of us. It seems he was no great fan of mine either.

Over the phone, John launched into a tirade about how poor my work, and my judgement, had been in allowing the

Committee to reach the decision it had made. He went on to accuse me of lacking enthusiasm for the visit and advising the Committee badly because of that. He was, he said, going to speak to the Clerk about me.

However much I explained the context – the lack of any formal approach, the postponement of the Committee meeting, how I'd tried to make alternative arrangements, and so on - John simply wouldn't listen.

I almost completely lost it. The pressures of managing the Committee's workload and internal relationships through the FMD crisis, now magnified by an ongoing and unnecessary dispute with the Department (which included my being spied upon), all came to a head at that moment.

Here was a Principal Clerk, whom I thought of as having successfully avoided all the high-pressure jobs and carved himself an 'easy number' niche, attacking me about my judgement, so soon after my members had expressly commended that judgement? How dare he?

I remember feeling the pulse throbbing in my head, my face reddening and my fists and teeth clenching really, really, hard. I even felt tears trying to make their way from my eyes. I had never felt so angry in a work situation. Frankly, it was lucky that John was on the phone, and not in my office.

I ended the call with an expletive-laden rant and a dramatic crashing down of the telephone handset, after which desk and office walls were thumped and knuckles mildly damaged.

Such rage! Looking back, these would probably now be considered classic symptoms of stress. I had been working nine, ten, eleven-hour days for many months (a lot for a career civil servant) with no recent personal time off, other than the one fateful Damien day.

It was also the case that my home life and relationships with my wife and young children were being affected, and I wasn't sleeping well. Back then, though, stress was just part of the job, and we were expected to 'get on with it'.

I channeled my rage into one of the most brutal emails I had ever sent in my working life, rejecting John's allegations and setting out my complaints about his handling of the situation. John told me later that he copied it to the Clerk.

I don't remember who I spoke to first after (almost) calming down. It was probably Joe, who had been further promoted from Clerk Assistant to 'Deputy Clerk designate' and whom I considered to be my real boss. He was somewhat more understanding (he was also no big fan of John's) and said he would try to smooth things over.

A couple of days later, on the Wednesday, I managed to get the Deputy Chairman to agree to host a small event, having established that he no longer had to visit Brussels. George had also been lobbied by Billy Armstrong (his party colleague) after I had spoken to Billy about my concerns.

Even that (apparent) solution caused more friction. John had, apparently, gone behind my back and approached George Savage himself. John then rang me again (sometime after 6.30

pm), presumably to 'set a trap', asking me how it had now come about that George was able to host an event.

After listening to my explanation, John then triumphantly announced that George had told him, in front of a witness, that it (John's conversation) was the first he'd heard of the Canadian visit. I told John that this was absolute nonsense, but it was clear he thought he had caught me out in a big lie.

Knowing George as I did ("and what are we doing today"), I was not surprised that he had attended both Committee meetings at which the visit had been discussed but remembered nothing about those discussions. I paid George another quick visit and refreshed his memory on the subject being raised at the two Committee meetings (showing him a copy of the minutes and draft minutes of each).

I then rang John back to put him right, offering him a copy of the minutes too. He declined, assuring me that he did not doubt my word. Hah! I was now even more raging, as I felt that John had potentially undermined my position with the Deputy Chairman. That said, I reckoned that none of this would bother George in the slightest.

Wiser heads must have become involved, and calmed both of us down, because I recall having a much more civil 'management meeting' with John on Thursday the 14th, at which no allegations were levelled, and no expletives used.

I reminded John that the newly appointed Clerks had been promised that there would be rotation of Clerking posts a year or so after our appointment and that this was now overdue.

John acknowledged that my position was more difficult than most, having been seconded from DARD, and that this should probably not have been allowed to happen. He did not, however, offer any timetable for staff moves.

In the end, the Deputy Chairman and four other Committee members attended the reception and buffet lunch on Friday the 15th. I also attended to support them as their Clerk, but I think John maybe took on some of the responsibility for the event, and he was able to involve the Speaker, some MLAs and senior Assembly officials too.

So, the Canadian visitors were well looked-after and happy, no diplomatic incident took place, and an open invitation was made to my members to visit the Canadian Senate. I wondered how long it might be before a visit to Canada was suggested.

My brutal email was never mentioned again, and I like to think that was because the Clerk saw that I had a point. I remained quietly livid with John, though, and made it my mission to avoid dealing with him if at all possible.

Chapter 35: The disappearing Duke

Some politicians have very sensitive political antennae. They can see which way the wind is blowing. They hear things. They avoid situations that might reflect badly on them.

Dr Paisley wasn't available to attend the next two Committee meetings – one before and one following the Easter recess – at which the Committee's position on formally demanding the attendance of the fisheries officials fell spectacularly apart. George Savage was left to chair both of these meetings.

The reader might think there is a connection between the previous two paragraphs. I couldn't possibly comment.

On the 22nd of March, the Committee considered a letter from the Speaker and also heard, in person, from the Assembly's legal adviser, Claire. It seemed that the Speaker could indeed issue a notice as requested by the Committee, but that he was reluctant to do so, not least because Claire considered it likely that the Department would seek a judicial review of the Speaker's use of this Statutory power.

Claire also felt that such a review was unlikely to find that the subject matter was sufficiently serious to warrant the use of that Power. There had been no 'smoking gun' found to suggest that the Committee had been misled. The only saving grace was that the Committee had received incomplete information on the operation of the 'Strike price' mechanism, but that was probably inadvertent, and there was really nothing else.

With the chief pot-stirrer not attending this meeting, and his son staying surprisingly quiet, the Committee deliberated at length, before agreeing further proposals which were to be put to the Minister as a way of resolving the dispute.

While I couched the resulting draft letter in as positive a way as I could for the Committee, it was apparent that the Committee was ready to back down, and George had to sign this letter on the Committee's behalf. He also had to write to the Speaker to keep him abreast of developments. He was not best pleased about doing either.

By the time Easter was over and the Committee met again on the 12th of April, the Minister had replied with some further thoughts. By now members (there were only six of them that day, both Paisleys and three others having sent apologies) were fed up with the whole thing, and they agreed that the matter must be brought to a conclusion.

They also agreed to effectively accept the Minister's terms, resolving that the Committee would:

- advise the Speaker that a notice under the Committee's Statutory powers was no longer sought;
- ask DARD to provide a worked example of how the 'Strike Price' would operate in practice within the decommissioning scheme;

- agree a list of members' questions on the Strike Price and on the scheme in general, which would be forwarded to DARD in advance of the next meeting; and
- agree to the Minister's proposal that the named fisheries officials would attend the next meeting and that members would limit themselves to asking the supplied questions only, with the officials providing answers to those questions.

Again, George had to be the signatory to the Committee's response to the Minister, and again he wasn't best pleased.

Far from flexing the Committee's big, statutory, muscles, members were now scrabbling round for a meaningless 'set piece' question session to mask their almost total surrender. I thought that this was, politically, quite humiliating, and I believe George also felt that quite keenly.

I had a new member of staff (Sean) attend his first meeting that day, as Jonathan's replacement (this time, happily, as a permanent, rather than agency, member of staff). I didn't think it was a great start for him to witness such a climbdown.

The set piece took place at the Committee's next meeting, held on the 19th of April, when Dr Paisley resumed the Chair.

It was beyond awkward. The Chairman moved to private session, and DARD's delegation trooped in, with Peter (the Staff Officer) surrounded by three of his most senior management, including the Permanent Secretary, like a cub under the Pride's protection. There was no sign of Jim, and I don't remember his absence being explained.

The Chairman was noticeably in quiet form. Members meekly asked the pre-supplied questions, Peter quietly answered them, then left the room. This took less than 20 minutes.

Senior management stayed on, and I minuted what followed as a "full and frank discussion" between them and my members. In Civil Service terms, that means it was a pretty feisty exchange.

Members were clearly not happy at their humiliation, and still (at least according to Dr Paisley) had a sense that they may have been duped or slighted in some way, while the senior officials weren't happy with what they saw as the Committee's attempted interference in the Department's internal staffing matters.

There wasn't a whole lot of agreement in those discussions, and the session ended with the Permanent Secretary undertaking to set out proposals for how future business might be handled between DARD and the Committee.

I let out a massive sigh of relief when that meeting ended. This issue had taken from the 8th of February to the 19th of April to resolve and had caused the team and me so much additional work.

Relationships had been quite badly damaged, purely (in my view) because of the petulance and questionable agenda of some fishermen's representatives, and the Chairman's predilection to the incitement of fury in others, then subsequent stubbornness in the face of the actual evidence.

The whole dispute did not represent Dr Paisley's 'finest hour', and I remember thinking that members would not be as quick to march up the hill behind him in future.

Chapter 36: They are really starting to annoy me now

All through the 'Fisheriesgate' period, the Committee's normal business continued, including finishing off the current Inquiry and making arrangements for the next.

During the 5th of March meeting, members had approved my draft findings and conclusions for the Rural Development Inquiry and had instructed me to draft the report accordingly.

At the 8th of March meeting, some of the farmer members sought to extend the FMD Inquiry to include wider animal disease prevention and control, given that issues had arisen recently in Northern Ireland with TB, Brucellosis and Botulism. I was sent off to revise the FMD Inquiry's Terms of Reference, the first version of which had already been the subject of a press release.

This was one of the many times where I could just have banged my head on the Committee table. Could they not have thought of this before they had gone public?

While I tried to revise the terms of reference as instructed, I wasn't at all happy with the way they looked, and I convinced members to defer consideration of them until after the Easter break.

It still felt like it was a constant battle for me to try to keep the Committee focused on the important over the trivial. Members were very easily distracted and still, after two-and-a-half years of the Committee's existence, desperately afraid of missing something about which they'd later be criticized.

Despite our previous discussions, Dr Paisley was no help at all in this regard, and he could flit very quickly from having a total absence of interest in a subject, to (with no apparent reason) becoming the greatest advocate of the Committee's involvement in it.

I did keep working on him, though, and at the meeting on the 22nd of March I got him to agree (and to convince other members) to prioritise what I saw as the most pressing issues.

We therefore went into the Easter recess with a manageable number of future agenda items and a tacit agreement that the Committee would 'gloss over' other matters for now.

As one of the agreed priorities, proper line-by-line consideration of the Rural Development Inquiry report began at the meeting held on the 19th of April, continued on the 26th and concluded at the meeting on the 3rd of May, when a draft motion for an Assembly debate was also agreed.

The 'take note' experiment for Committee reports must have been dropped by then, as the motion was for the Assembly to endorse the report and to call on the Minister to implement recommendations relevant to her department.

Also, on the 19th of April, members agreed terms of reference for a separate animal disease Inquiry to run in parallel with the FMD one that that already been announced. I had tried, but I simply couldn't make the two matters into a coherent subject for one Inquiry. Through my usual channels (probably Ian Junior on this occasion) I had secured Dr Paisley's support for this approach ahead of the meeting.

It wasn't ideal to try to run parallel Inquiries, but I thought it could be done in a way similar to the Committee's consideration of the Pigs and Beef sectors alongside the retailers as part of an overall debt Inquiry, so I was reasonably confident it could be done.

Running these particular inquiries at the same time also made sense as the same officials and industry stakeholders were involved in both subjects, and we could therefore 'kill two birds' as they gave evidence.

The Committee meeting on the 3rd of May was to be Bertie's last, and members wished him well in his new post. I had got on really well with Bertie and appreciated all he did for the team. I had thought (and hoped) that we were going to be a settled team for a while after Sean had joined us, but, as I recall, Bertie had secured a promotion in his parent department, so there was no standing in the way of his progress.

A new Assistant Clerk, Joanne, joined the team and attended her first meeting on Friday the 10th of May. A bit of gender balance wouldn't do us any harm, I thought.

The Minister had appeared before the Committee on the 3rd of May, but it was proving difficult to secure further dates up to the summer recess. John Dallat once again challenged the need for the Committee to meet on a Friday, and I was once again charged with making enquiries about making a change.

I was, frankly, a little fed up with this 'same old, same old' complaint, and I knew what my answer would be. No other Committee would move its meeting to the Friday, and there were no spaces in the weekly calendar into which we could insert the Agriculture Committee meeting. I wanted to say, "Just get over it, John", but obviously I couldn't.

I went through the motions, reported as expected, and during the meeting on the 10th of May the Committee agreed to retain the status quo.

Also, during the 10th of May meeting, the Committee met with DARD officials in relation to its proposed regulations on TSEs. Members' ears would always 'prick up' when this subject arose, as they hadn't quite got over having paid out public money for Frank the consultant to tell them nothing of any use about it.

The discussions on TSEs that day included the issue of the burial of ash in registered landfill sites from incineration of 'specified risk materials'. I think it was during this session (although it could conceivably have happened at the time of Frank's failed advice) that Billy Armstrong came off with what may have been his most memorable contribution.

There had been discussions about the need to destroy the 'prions' in infected material (e.g., animals with BSE) which could cause transmission of TSEs to humans. This was, apparently, proving difficult to achieve.

It came to Billy's turn to speak, and he said something akin to:

"You know the way they said that these prions can only be got rid of by very high temperatures? Well, what are the hottest things we have on this earth? Volcanoes! Is the answer not to put these dead animals into volcanoes? That would get rid of your prions".

Even with Billy's reputation for some 'left field' remarks, this one caught everyone by surprise. No-one said a word, which made the Chairman's 'stage whisper' to me seem audible to all: "Mister Clerk, is Billy being serious, or is he having a laugh?"

I got no help from Billy's expression. "I think, Chairman, that he's being perfectly serious" I replied, shaking my head in disbelief, then realizing that my disbelief shouldn't be quite so obvious to the room.

Without blinking, the Chairman said: "Ok. Thanks for that, Billy, though I'm not sure that's quite the answer" and he moved swiftly on. Volcanoes were, unsurprisingly, never mentioned again.

I had another interesting involvement during the 10th of May meeting.

Called by the Chairman to speak, Gardiner Kane announced that he had a statement to make to the Committee. Perhaps he was back in Dr Paisley's good books, I thought, since this was quite unusual. Gardiner's demeanour was such that it seemed clear he felt this was his 'big moment', and he began to read out words from a page that he had, apparently, carefully prepared.

The issue was, he said, relevant to the Committee's recent LMC Inquiry report and he wanted to ask the Committee to examine a witness (whom he named) who would 'blow the whistle' on a practice of changing meat gradings after the formal classification had taken place. Gardiner then alleged that this had happened in a specific meat plant.

Something clicked in my head, and I quickly asked the Chairman to stop him from saying any more. I drew members' attention to a letter from the Minister that was in their packs for that day. In the letter, there was an indication that the very matter being raised by Gardiner may be before the Courts, and the issue would then be 'sub judice' and therefore not in order for discussion in open session.

While I was reluctant to rain on Gardiner's parade, my duty, as Clerk, to protect the Committee took precedence. The Chairman took my advice, allowed no further discussion, and instructed me to check this point in time for next week's meeting. Gardiner's moment had passed, and his deflation was visible.

As it turned out, I reported at the meeting on the 17th of May that while the matter was not yet at hearing, a charge had been laid against the meat plant by the DPP and the matter was indeed sub judice. With that news, most of the Committee appreciated my having intervened the previous week, but I got the impression that Gardiner was not terribly happy, despite my having saved him potential grief.

Just when I was relieved about one issue disappearing, another one arrived, when, at the meeting on the 17th of May, members discussed the closure of a prawn factory in Kilkeel.

Members were most exercised about this, but the DARD Minister had, I thought correctly, informed the Committee that this was a matter for the Minister of Enterprise, Trade and Investment (ETI) and therefore not her responsibility.

Dr Paisley didn't let that reality get in the way, and, at his suggestion, the Committee agreed to put the 'Strasbourg three' back together and have the Chairman, Deputy Chairman and PJ Bradley meet the other Department's Minister.

I tried to convince the Chairman that this was going well beyond his Committee's statutory remit, but he was having none of it, citing the reliance of fishermen on having access to such processing facilities for their catch.

He had a point, but so did I. Our Committee should not be scrutinizing the work of another department, particularly when they had more than enough work to do in scrutinizing their own.

I had really started to notice that my tolerance of some of the Committee members had waned over the time that I'd spent with them. Their lack of understanding of issues, the quality of some of their contributions, their lack of preparation for meetings, and their seeming reluctance to stop flogging a dead horse were all things that caused me irritation.

It also seemed to me that I was having less and less influence on Dr Paisley and his chairmanship of the Committee. I was sure I wasn't the first to find working with him frustrating, but I was very concerned that he wasn't listening as closely to my advice as he once did. I wasn't at all sure that he was as enthusiastic about the whole Committee set-up as he had once been.

Perhaps I needed to get to the Summer recess. Perhaps there was more to it. All I knew was that I just couldn't quite shake my annoyance with them all, and that I had begun to long for a change of scenery.

There had been a second, and more substantial, arms move by the IRA in April, so I was slightly more hopeful for the future of the Assembly as a whole.

For that reason, I don't believe that I was actively trying to return to my parent Department (if they'd even have taken me back) but I had begun to think that the once-promised rotation of staff might offer a possible 'escape' from this particular Chair and this group of members, and from the way I was feeling at that time.

Chapter 37: George sticks closely to the script and summer approaches

Monday the 20th of May saw the Assembly plenary debate on the Committee's Inquiry report: 'Preparation for the next phase of the Rural Development Programme (2001-2006)'[45]. Joanne was with me in the Officials' Box for the first time.

The Chairman was not available that day, so George Savage moved the motion and opened the debate. He managed pretty well with the speaking notes that I had provided for him, and these were essentially a re-working of some of the highlights of the report's Executive Summary.

He added his own remark at the end of his delivery of my notes, commending the report to the Assembly as an example of good scrutiny. He is right, I thought, in a moment of self-congratulation. It probably was.

I was happy that the opening speech had gone well, and that George had covered most of the key points. PJ Bradley spoke next, and I was quietly pleased when he remarked that George hadn't left much for the rest of the Committee to say.

It was also nice to hear Ian Paisley junior, who spoke after PJ, giving "particular thanks to the Clerk of the Committee and

---

[45] Official Report Bound Volume 16 pages 170-181

his staff, whose expertise greatly assisted us". As per usual, Ian Junior then managed to find something to criticize (the size of DARD's Rural Development budget allocation) but his criticism was fairly mild.

There were few surprises within the other three contributions from Committee members, or in the now expected contribution from 'big gun' Jim Shannon. By and large, members' focus was on trying to include the farming community in the second phase of the Rural Development programme: something that hadn't happened in its first phase.

There was also an element of déjà vu from previous debates on the Committee's reports: Gerry McHugh suggested that there should be far more emphasis placed on the North/South aspects of rural development; Billy Armstrong left me trying to make sense of what he was saying, and John Dallat praised the Minister for what she was already doing.

John, of course, had a particular interest in the rural development programme, with his involvement in the Kilrea project, and I understood perfectly where he was coming from when he expressed his hope and expectation that community groups availing of future funding wouldn't be faced with the same difficulties that had surrounded early projects.

He was particularly scathing about consultants not fully appraising the viability of projects and offering poor advice to community groups, then not staying around to help address their difficulties. The experience at Kilrea had clearly affected him. I found myself nodding in agreement, which didn't happen often where John was concerned.

The Minister gave her response which, again, held few surprises, although she seemed to recognize that the Committee's recommendations had been constructive.

It was left, then, for George to give his response and bring the debate to a close. I had rejected any thought of trying (from the Officials' Box) to supply George with updates in 'real time' in response to members' and the Minister's contributions, as I was concerned this would be difficult for us both.

But I had also tried to forecast what the Minister's response might be and had explained to George (just before the debate) how I had provided some additional points for him to make if she took some of the lines that I was expecting her to.

I had specifically identified farmers' form-filling and development services as one such issue, and, sure enough, the Minister's response had suggested these weren't really a problem that the Department needed to address.

The speaking notes I had given George were printed off in bold, black, type, and the font was sized 16 for easy reading. I had explained to him that I'd included his additional 'steers' (or lines to take) in italic, red, type sized 8 and in separate paragraphs to the main speaking notes in order to differentiate them.

As I sat in the Box, I just hoped that George would pick up on the Minister's comments and deploy the response I'd provided, but there was no sign of that. His summing up followed my notes pretty well, at first, with only a few personal 'Georgeisms' added.

He then followed the notes a little too well, with him saying something like:

"The Committee has carried out a thorough Inquiry, and has offered a report worthy of the Assembly's endorsement. Only use the following paragraph if the Minister does not agree to provide development services to farmers. The Committee was concerned that no help was offered to farmers, a specific target group, to fill in forms."

Big black bold text? Small red text? It had made no difference. I think George then paused, realizing that something wasn't quite right. He said a final few words, then sat down.

My eyes closed so no-one could see them rolling, and I dropped my head below the level of the railing at the front of the Officials' box to hide the look of embarrassment and despair on my face.

I then glanced around the Chamber checking for the inevitable titters of merriment at George's expense. But there were none. It was nearly 6.15 and there were very few in the Chamber. Those that were present looked almost comatose after the hour-and-a-half debate. They hadn't noticed. He'd actually got away with it!

289

The motion was passed without any division, and it was time for home, but not before I had run to the Hansard office to see what could be done.

Colleagues there had already spotted George's gaffe, and they assured me they would strategically omit the offending sentence when the Official Report was produced the next day. They had to do this fairly regularly, I believe. I know this approach resulted in a more coherent read, but the devil in me almost wished that they didn't.

I expected the Inquiry report debate to be the last 'big ticket' item for the Committee before the Summer. It pretty much was, although there was the Committee Stage of a small DARD Bill to deal with (a Bill to prohibit the keeping of animals primarily for slaughter for their fur).

I wasn't expecting any contention around that Bill in the Committee and there was none, with members agreeing their final report at the 5th of July meeting, the last to be held in the 2001/2002 session.

The future Inquiry into the FMD outbreak was still causing a few issues. Members wanted to have some external research done on the subject, but they didn't really know what that research should include. I made something up that I thought might be suitable, and members agreed draft terms of reference for the research and instructed me to seek proposals before Summer recess.

I was also instructed to consult with the Assembly's recently appointed Procurement Officer before any call for proposals went out.

Dr Paisley didn't seem particularly engaged in any of these matters. Gate fever, perhaps, or something more?

Finally, the Committee agreed on the makeup of an assessment panel to consider whatever proposals were received for the research project. PJ, Gerry and George were to join the Chairman on this (nicely balanced) panel, and I was looking forward to seeing how the personal interactions between Gerry and the Doc might work in the smaller forum.

The plan was to take oral evidence for the FMD Inquiry in September, so my team and I would have to work on organizing that during recess too, which was a bit annoying.

While all this was going on, one member (I think Gardiner Kane) suggested that the Committee should undertake a further Inquiry into the Dairy Sector. I think that the tone of my response may have betrayed my frustration, as I pointed out that the Committee had already agreed to run two Inquiries in parallel, and very firmly suggested that those Inquiries should be completed before embarking on another. That seemed to do the trick, and nothing further was said.

Any hope I had that the Committee might have forgotten about the closure of the prawn processing plant was dashed at the Committee's last meeting, held on the 5th of July.

Members heard evidence that day from a delegation from the Newry and Mourne District Council, the local Trade Union and from yet another ANIFPO delegation.

Yes, I could see that the loss of 143 jobs was a real problem for the area, but no, I couldn't see that it was any business of the Agriculture and Rural Development Committee.

This was a commercial decision by a private company to relocate its operations to Scotland. For all the politicians' bluster (and I understood their need to be seen to be involved), it was my view that sometimes these things couldn't be helped.

They almost certainly wouldn't (or shouldn't) be influenced by a Committee whose function was to scrutinize the work of a Department that had no responsibility for the company's business or the resulting job losses. I said as much to the Dr Paisley, both privately beforehand, and aloud in the Committee room.

Again, my advice fell on deaf ears, and, with much encouragement from the Chairman, the Committee further agreed to participate in a 'task force' which was to be made up of the Council, the Union, ANIFPO and the Committee (with the Chairman, Deputy Chairman, PJ Bradley and Billy Armstrong all agreeing to play a part).

I thought that this was likely to be 'all talk' from the members, and was not likely to materialize, as I knew that they relished summer recess at least as much as I did.

I was exasperated and resolved to extricate myself from any involvement if the task force did go ahead, on the grounds that it wasn't legitimate Committee business. Let them get involved as MLAs if they must, I thought, although I wasn't looking forward to the argument I thought I would be likely to have with the Chairman on that point.

As the Chairman brought the final meeting of the 2001/2002 session to a close, and the Committee agreed to meet again on Friday the 6th of September, my usual sigh of relief for reaching recess was somewhat tempered by the work that still lay ahead over the next number of weeks.

I was not in good form at all.

Chapter 38: Time for reflection and time to go

I didn't rush into any decisions, and I diligently did my duty in tying up as many loose ends as possible for the Committee, including getting the Committee's Committee Stage report on the Fur Farming Bill printed.

I also met with the Assembly's Procurement Officer, as instructed, and he convinced me that it would not be appropriate to issue a call for proposals from external researchers under the terms of reference that had been agreed. I can't really remember why, but I wasn't, frankly, too disappointed at that outcome, and I reckoned it could all wait until the Committee returned.

As I had forecast, the Committee members' supposed involvement in the prawn plant 'task force' came to nought, and I had nothing further to do with the issue. Somewhat ironically, I subsequently found out that the prawn processor's operations, having been moved to Scotland, were then moved to China a few years later.

Over the early part of the Summer break, I thought long and hard about my own position. I couldn't escape the feeling that I was damaging my future prospects in my parent department by virtue of my (apparently) playing for the opposing team.

There was no doubt that I was conflicted. It was part of my job to identify flaws in what the Department did, and in the information it provided to the Committee, but sometimes this would reflect badly on former colleagues, and that was hard.

That was probably the most critical context for my deliberations, although I also felt that my enthusiasm for Committee work had waned. I was no longer as keen as I had been to service these particular members, with whom I'd worked closely for approaching three years, and I was much less tolerant of their faults. That pained me, as I always wanted to give of my very best, professionally, and serving the members diligently was a crucial aspect of my role.

I also needed to consider my relationship with the Chairman. I did not expect to be able to control Dr Paisley – many before me had tried and failed – but I did get the sense that he was responding less well to the advice that I was giving him than he had earlier on. I was not looking for a personal friendship - I knew I was 'Mister Clerk' with a job to do - but I thought that the 'visiting Jim' episode might have affected his level of trust in me personally, and I knew it was vital for there to be a high degree of mutual trust between Clerk and Chair.

I felt that if I was to move on, the long summer recess would be the least disruptive time for me to do that, and for the team to get used to that prospect. My team appeared pretty settled, as we had had no changes in personnel since mid-May. Joanne had proved a more than capable replacement for Bertie as Assistant Clerk, and she was getting to grips with the varied and heavy workload that the Committee created for itself. Sean had proven himself to be every bit as good in his Clerical Supervisor role as I had hoped.

I was conscious, however, that John was unhappy, having missed out on promotion to the role of Clerical Supervisor. He had applied for the promotion competition but had been ruled ineligible even for the interview stage, despite being one of the best Clerical Officers the Assembly had on its books. I thought it possible that John would move on as a result, even though he liked the work, and he had a great relationship with colleagues.

So, there was a question mark over whether or not I could actually engineer a move. While I was able to remind my management of the promises made about rotating staff, I also believed that none of my colleagues was actively looking for a change.

I kept at it, however, and after everyone had taken their Summer annual leave and recharged somewhat, I eventually 'wore down' the senior team and arrangements were finally made for me to move to the Assembly's Business Office, where I would work initially with the Assembly Questions process.

I found out that my colleague Cathie White, who worked for another Committee, would be my replacement and I wondered if she would get called 'Missus Clerk' by the Chairman.

The two sets of Chairs and Deputy Chairs were alerted to the changes (which came into operation on the 2nd of September) by the Clerk Assistant and the Deputy Clerk, so I never got to say any formal 'goodbyes' to Dr Paisley, Mr Savage and the rest of my members in the Committee setting.

That was a pity, in some ways. While certain members had certainly begun to annoy me, we had been through quite a journey together as a group, and I expected that I would remember them with fondness (as I do now). I hoped they would all feel the same way.

I was very happy, therefore, when my attention was drawn to the introduction to the formal minutes of proceedings of the Committee's meeting of the 6th of September 2002 which said:

"The Committee placed on formal record its thanks to Mr. Paul Moore for his hard work and dedication and agree that the Chairman should write expressing members' gratitude to Mr. Moore".

I remember receiving Dr Paisley's letter and putting it in a drawer in the Business Office for safekeeping, but I'm afraid it got lost in one of the many moves of office and job that I made since then. Not to worry. My tenure as the Committee's (and Dr Paisley's) Clerk is immortalized in those (and earlier) Minutes of Proceedings for the Committee.

I wondered how they'd all get on 'under new management'. But as it happened, Dr Paisley's Committee only existed for six meetings without me.

In October 2002, police raided Sinn Fein's offices at Stormont, and arrested the party's head of administration,

Denis Donaldson, a former IRA prisoner. It was alleged at the time that he was part of an IRA 'spy ring' that was operating within Stormont, although charges were later dropped.[46]

As a result of the raid, the DUP pulled its two Ministers from the Executive on the 11th of October, with the UUP threatening to do the same on the following Tuesday if Sinn Fein was not excluded from office by the Secretary of State. Rather than doing that, the SoS suspended the Assembly on the 14th of October, and re-imposed direct rule in Northern Ireland.

That was it for the Assembly, and its Committees, for several years. When it did return in proper, devolved, format, the political landscape had changed further still.

The DUP's and Dr Paisley's approach of 'riding two horses' (i.e., continued opposition to the Institutions at the same time as participation in them) proved highly successful, with two Assembly elections in the intervening period confirming the DUP as the Assembly's largest party.

Indeed, the 2007 Assembly election result allowed Dr Paisley to complete his personal and political evolution when the former firebrand minister of "Never" was appointed to be Northern Ireland's First Minister, after which he went on to form his 'chuckle brothers' relationship with Sinn Fein's Martin McGuinness. Back in 1999, such an outcome would have been unthinkable, and I firmly believe that it only

---

[46] Source: Wikipedia entry on 'Stormontgate' read on the 23rd of June 2020

became possible because of his tenure as Chairman of the Committee.

It was clearly hard for Dr Paisley, during this period, to rise above his baser instincts and to behave in a fair and inclusive manner to opponents, some of which he considered to be enemies. It is true that Dr Paisley reverted to type on many occasions, but it is my belief that his Committee work enabled him to see these enemies more as human beings, with whom, in the right context, he could find some common ground.

I also think that this period confirmed to Dr Paisley that his leadership and influence could travel beyond his usual constituency and that participation in 'the system' did not result in the sky falling down in the form of electoral losses or failure. Quite the opposite in fact, and I am certain that helped bring him, and his party, to the table and, ultimately, to the St. Andrews Agreement and the Assembly's restoration.

With hindsight, however, I would have to question whether the 'two horses' approach laid sufficient foundations for the party's longer-term ability to work constructively with Sinn Fein. On recent evidence, it seems not.

But we weren't to know that at the time. All I knew, even then, was that I had been fortunate to have worked alongside such a famous (and perhaps infamous) political character. When I had heard Dr Paisley nominating himself as Chairman, I had anticipated an interesting ride, and it had certainly been that for the best part of three years.

The Summer of 2002 was, however, the right time for me to move on from that work, and I enjoyed several more years with the Assembly, which included a couple of external secondments during the long Assembly suspension from 2002 to 2007. I came across Dr Paisley and many of the other former Committee members quite frequently in my remaining years, both in the Questions office and as a Clerk to the Business Committee.

I then returned to the Department in 2008, a spell which included an appearance before the Agriculture Committee, when I locked horns (and fell out quite badly) with the DUP's William McCrea, who by then was Chairman. It seemed I hadn't learned the necessary charm after all!

I moved on to the Health and Safety Executive (HSENI) in 2011, eventually retiring in September 2019.

Mine was a fairly long, and not particularly distinguished, career. But now, when people ask me what I worked at before I retired, I am delighted to tell them that I was a boring Civil Servant for many years, but that for just a little while I worked alongside a very famous politician, and he called me "Mister Clerk".

The End

Appendix: 'Cast List' of officials relevant to Statutory Committees 1999-2002

Clerking roles in the Assembly were developed in line with equivalent roles in the House of Commons at Westminster. In the early days of the Assembly, a Committee team normally comprised a Clerk, an Assistant Clerk, an Executive Support officer and (sometimes) an Admin Support officer.

Clerk Assistant: The most senior official with responsibilities for Clerking Services. The CA answered to the Deputy Clerk and ultimately to the Clerk. The Clerk Assistant supported the Speaker 'at Table' in the Assembly Chamber as well as having senior administrative responsibilities. This post was considered equivalent to NI Civil Service Assistant Secretary (Unified Grade 5) level.

Principal Clerk of Committees: Answerable to the Clerk Assistant, the postholder was responsible for 'the Committee Office', which in turn serviced the needs of, and ensured consistency of approach across, the Assembly's Statutory and Standing Committees. From time to time, the post-holder also Clerked a Standing Committee.

Committee Clerk: The Clerk was responsible for the provision of advice and support to each Committee's Chair, Deputy Chair and members, undertaking research and providing timely and accurate briefs, preparing draft Committee reports, speeches and press releases, and liaison with press, media, government departments, private and voluntary organisations and the public. This was considered equivalent to Civil Service Principal Officer (Grade 7) level.

Assistant Clerk: The Assistant Clerk was responsible for assisting the Clerk in his or her duties and was the direct line manager for the Committee's Executive Support (or Clerical Supervisor). The Assistant Clerk would ordinarily draft the minutes of proceedings for each Committee meeting and be responsible for ensuring the issue of members' papers in time for meetings. This post was considered equivalent to Civil Service Staff Officer level.

Executive Support (became known as Clerical Supervisor): The Executive Support Officer or Clerical Supervisor was responsible for collating members' papers for Committee meetings, and for various administrative tasks within each Committee team. The Clerical Supervisor also acted as line manager for the Administrative Support officers (or Clerical Officers). This role was considered equivalent to the Civil Service 'EO II' grade.

Administrative Support (became known as Clerical Officer): Clerical Officers had to perform administrative tasks as instructed by their supervisors. This included copying, filing and (in Dr Paisley's Committee) providing the Chairman with his tea. This was equivalent to the Civil Service Administrative Officer grade.

Author

I P Moore (known as Paul) is a retired civil servant, who lives with his family in Bangor, Co. Down.

His career included nine years seconded to the Northern Ireland Assembly, where he was responsible for drafting the text in the 'Assembly Companion' (a book on rulings, conventions and practice) as well as several Committee reports. This is his first book as author.

After a cancer diagnosis and treatment in 2012/2013, he drew up an extensive bucket list. Items on the list included cycling 100k, appearing on a national TV game show, swimming 5000m in a lake and writing a book. He has now achieved all of these but has plenty more to do.

Printed in Great Britain
by Amazon

84093592R00180